HOW TO BECOME A
MILLIONAIRE FUEL DEALER

SUCCESS AND FAILURE FACTORS OF OPERATING A FUEL FRANCHISE

BY JOHNSTONE CHIKWANDA- PhD.

HOW TO BECOME A
MILLIONAIRE FUEL DEALER

SUCCESS AND FAILURE FACTORS OF OPERATING A FUEL FRANCHISE

BY JOHNSTONE CHIKWANDA- PhD.

Copyright © 2022 by Johnstone Chikwanda

You can connect with the author at:

LinkedIn: https://www.linkedin.com/in/johnstone-c-44229088/
Facebook: https://www.facebook.com/Johnstonechikwanda.zm/

No parts of the publication may be reproduced, distributed, or transmitted in any form or by any means including photocopying, recording, or other electronic or mechanical methods without prior written permission from the author.

ISBN: 979-8356-446443

HOW TO BECOME A
MILLIONAIRE FUEL DEALER

*SUCCESS AND FAILURE FACTORS
OF OPERATING A FUEL FRANCHISE*

BY JOHNSTONE CHIKWANDA- PhD.

DEDICATION

This book is dedicated to workers, investors and those who intend to invest in the oil industry.

ACKNOWLEDGEMENTS

Success has many mothers. This book is a result of strenuous research work part of which informed post graduate research work at my master's degree level. First and foremost, I humbly acknowledge and thank the source of my strength and inspiration to complete this book.

Secondly, I wish to thank my mentors, family and friends for the considerable support rendered to me not just at research stage but also at book writing stage.

I thank employees and fuel franchisees of Sasol, BP, Shell, Caltex, Total, and Engen for the support rendered to me during my research work. Without honest feedback from the franchisees, it would have been difficult to harvest success and failure factors in the fuel retail business. Furthermore, I extend my gratitude to the Fuel Retailers Association (FRA) for the interviews, published material and authors of other sources of secondary data which fed into my literature review.

I also wish to acknowledge the efforts of everyone who contributed in one way or another to my studies and subsequently to the success of this book.

I will be failing in my duty if I do not express my gratitude to my graphic designers, editors, book reviewers, typists and all those who provided oversight during this book project.

TABLE OF CONTENTS

11 | Foreword

13 | Chapter 1: Introduction

13 | 1.1 Introduction
14 | 1.2 Background to the Research
17 | 1.3 Reason for the research
17 | 1.4 Aim of the study
17 | 1.5 Objectives of the study
19 | 1.6 Research questions
19 | 1.7 Significance of the research

21 | Chapter 2

21 | 2.1 Introduction
21 | 2.2 Problems of owning a franchise
22 | 2.3 Franchised fuel business
23 | 2.4 The challenges of operating a franchise fuel business
26 | 2.5 Causes of fuel business collapse
33 | 2.6 Conclusion

35 | Chapter 3

35 | 3.1 Target Population for the research
35 | 3.2 The research instrument which was used to conduct the research
36 | 3.3 Data analysis of the research
36 | 3.4 Ensuring validity and reliability

39 | Chapter 4: Statement of Results, Discussion and Interpretation

39 | Introduction
39 | Sample characteristics
40 | Demographic profile of franchisees
75 | Interpretation and discussion

81 | Chapter 5: Conclusions and Recommendations

81 | 5.1 Introduction
81 | 5.2 Findings from the study
82 | 5.2.1 Findings from the literature review
84 | 5.2.2 Findings from the Primary Research
84 | 5.2.2.1 Demographic information
84 | 5.2.2.1.1 Gender involvement in the industry
85 | 5.2.2.2 Years of experience in fuel business
85 | 5.2.2.3 Number of previous dealers
86 | 5.2.2.4 Challenges of operating in the retail fuel business
92 | 5.2.2.5 Dealing with challenges in the retail sector
98 | 5. 2.2.6 Key success factors in retail fuel business
104 | 5.2.2.7 Major failure factors in the retail fuel sector
110 | 5.2.2.8 Summary of findings
111 | 5.2.2.9 Conclusion

113 | Bibliography

FOREWORD

This book is a product of rigorous business research in the downstream segment of the oil industry. The study was conducted on an adequate sample size in the Republic of South Africa which had about 5,000 petrol stations at the time of study. Petrol stations are also called garages, filling stations or gas stations depending on jurisdiction. The purpose of the research was to identify key success and failure factors in the fuel franchise industry.

After analysing secondary data from various publications, it was noted that the number of petrol stations had declined significantly not just in South Africa but also in other major countries such as the United States of America (USA) and United Kingdom (UK) at the time of the research. To this end, the author embarked on investigating the root causes of the sharp decline within my target population. Hence the aim stated above.

There is little independent information on the retail fuel business covering the challenges faced, success and failure factors. The oil industry is a government regulated industry, with government controlling not just the prices but also when to increase them. Government establishes both oil company and dealer margins. This is what makes investing in the oil business a delegate undertaking.

The author has identified and graphically presented success and failure factors. It is my considered view that all franchisees, captains of the industry, scholars, policy makers, investors including potential investors and those interested in knowing about the business world of fuel trading will find this book helpful.

The author has done his best to highlight what makes millionaires while others give up or become bankrupt in the same industry. The success factors elucidated in this book can also be utilised in other business settings.

CHAPTER 1:

INTRODUCTION

1.1 Introduction

There is a perception that operating a petrol station is lucrative. Therefore, many people all over the world and not just in South Africa dream of operating a famous petrol /gas station franchise. The prestige and other trophies of life that presumably accompany petrol franchise owners leaves the wider society bewildered and entrenched in the feeling that fuel business is indeed the popular black gold, an escape into the secluded wealthy class and a terminator of financial squalor and hopelessness.

However, others are successful, not many are fortunate. The number of petrol stations which have closed is quite high. Many dealers have gone out of business. Oil companies repossess petrol stations quite often and give them to others. It is frightening to see so many petrol stations advertised for sale in both print and electronic media. The industry despite being so lucrative appears fraught with a myriad of challenges. Therefore, a proper understanding of these challenges is a critical task for someone to survive in the industry.

This book is a product of an MBA study which investigated the challenges of owning a franchise fuel station. The information collected from the research is valuable to all those already operating petrol stations, those who intend to enter the industry and other stakeholders. By knowing ahead of time from an independent source what challenges exist, one is likely to brace for the challenges and how to navigate them. Not only did the study focus on the shortcoming of operating a franchise fuel station but also investigated what makes some franchisees successful and what makes others collapse.

1.2 Background to the Research

The research focussed on investigating challenges of owning a franchise in the fuel industry. This came in the wake of hundreds of sustained adverts of petrol stations being sold (Peacock Consulting, 2004). This industry is a lucrative one but why have so many stations changed hands or closed? What is even more worrying is that they are not new stations but old ones from all brands of fuel companies.
According to online encyclopedia, there were 18,000 petrol stations in the UK in 1992. By 2007, the number had dropped to 9,271. In Canada, there were 20,000 petrol stations in 1989. As at 2008, 12, 684 were in operation. In the United States of America, petrol stations also called gas stations are being shuttered at an accelerating dip; their numbers dropping by almost 3000 over the past 12 months (Wall Street Journal, July 8 2008). These closures stretch across the country from New York State which lost 200 gas stations over the past year, to North Dakota, which lost more than 130. Not too long ago, the biggest oil company in the world Exxon Mobil Corp said it planned to sell its 2,220 stations in the US. Other oil companies have already shed most of theirs (NPN Magazine, 2008:1). In a nutshell, there were 200,000 gas stations in the USA in 1994. As of 2008, 161, 368 were operational (NPN Magazine, 2008) According to a BBC News article titled "Mysterious death of the petrol station (BBC News, March 2008:1), it is understood

that since 2002, petrol stations in the UK have been shutting at an average rate of 600 a year. According to the trade body, the Petrol Retailers Associations of UK, there are now fewer people selling fuel to motorists than at any time since 1912.

It is not just the closure of stations across the world including South Africa but stations exchange hands several times meaning that either franchisees give up or they lose the franchise for various reasons. Cyrus Business Brokers, an association of professional business brokers specialising exclusively in the sale of petrol stations throughout South Africa recently reported on their website that they have a large inventory of petrol stations for sale. As of 24th January, 2012 the website had 456 petrol stations from almost all oil companies (Cyrus Business Brokers, 2012:1). This is just one site. There are other websites with a remarkable number of petrol stations for sale. What is even more worrying is that they are not newly built stations but old ones.

Furthermore, oil companies frequently repossess petrol stations and advertise for new dealers to come on board or close them down (Nigeria's Daily Trust, Friday January 1, 2010). It appears that either some dealers give up on their own due to various challenges or they lose the franchise license due to different reasons. Several of them have lost their investment in this industry. This retail fuel network across the country employs more than 50,000 pump attendants (Thomas, 2005:46). Whenever a station closes, it means that there is loss of employment. This is a major concern for the government given the high rate of unemployment in the country.

In addition, Small and Medium Enterprises (SMEs) such as franchise fuel dealers contribute to the gross domestic product (GDP). The SME national segment contributes a staggering portion of the overall GDP. Therefore, it is a setback whenever an entrepreneur goes out of business. Additionally, each time a petrol station closes; it affects motorists and the community that was being served by that particular station. The oil company, the franchisee, employees, government and other stakeholders all lose out. In keeping with Saunders, Lewis and Thornhill (2003: 2), the research outcome will help address real business issues and provide a process for solving managerial problems. It is therefore very critical to identify key parameters, and a matrix of defined challenges being faced in the industry. These challenges could form a proper basis of lobbying Departments of Energy (DoE). The function of the DoE is to regulate the Energy sector and determine margins available to the oil company (The Department of Minerals and Energy Report, 2004:1). I wish to underscore that the issue of a fixed margin regardless of the size and location of the station can become a serious source of financial malaise and lead to business failure for many franchisees.

Interested parties such as industry bodies will find the findings of the study useful. More often than not, potential investors wishing to invest in petrol stations have little access to useful information on how to survive and excel in the industry. It could that there is either little information or presenters of such opportunities present biased information without affording people an opportunity to look at the other picture. The other scenario could be that potential franchisees are so blinded by the perceived big money opportunity of the industry that they pay less attention to challenges of the industry.

It is the aforementioned backdrop that saved as a plank for the research work.

1.3 Reason for the research

The research was an investigation into the success and failure of operating a franchise fuel business in the Gauteng Province of the Republic of South Africa. Recent and old media reports have continued to reveal a worrying pattern of several petrol stations going out of business or getting listed for sale. A casual perusal on leading online advertisement shows several hundreds of petrol stations listed for sale or leasing from almost all major brands. It is a common phenomenon to see oil companies repossessing petrol stations from ailing dealers. This is despite the fact that the fuel industry is one of the most lucrative sectors in the world.

Therefore, several questions ought to be answered as to why so many old stations close down and others are listed for sale or lease. When a station closes down, it inconveniences the community it was servicing. Furthermore, both the oil company and the dealer loses business. This has an effect on the GDP of the country. Additionally, it leads to job losses. To this end, understanding the challenges could help reshape the approach to handling this sector by several stakeholders.

1.4 Aim of the study

The purpose of the research was to identify key success and failure factors in the retail fuel industry in the Gauteng Province, South Africa. The findings could be generalised over the fuel franchising industry if not the entire franchising world.

1.5 Objectives of the study

Objectives of the research were achieved through examining

secondary data from industry studies or publications and from primary data on the subject matter. Questionnaires were circulated to randomly selected fuel dealers.

The following were the specific objectives:

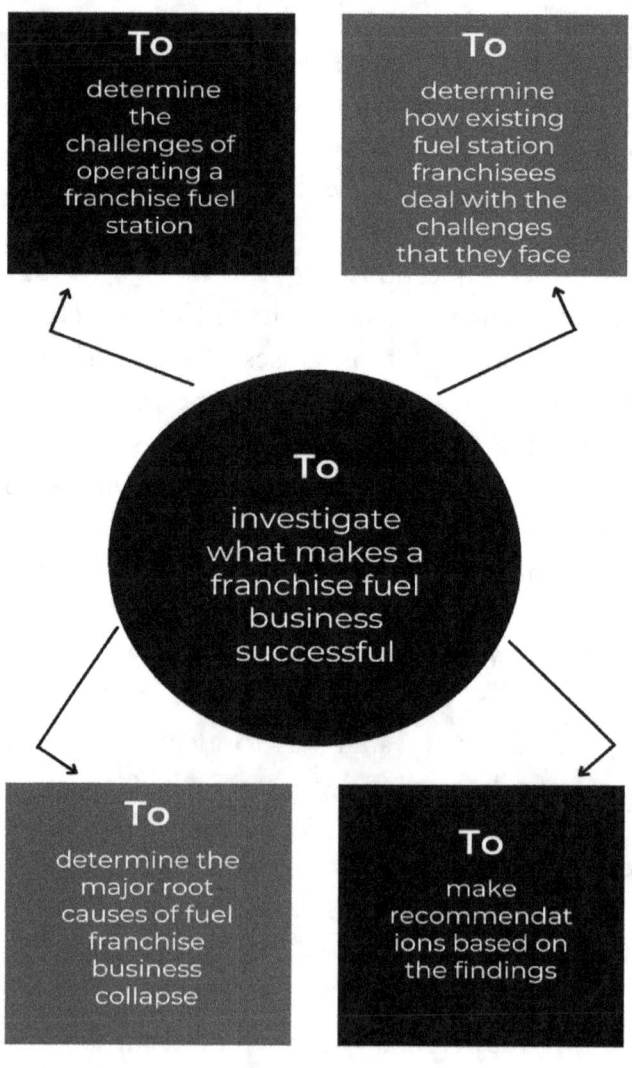

1.6 Research questions

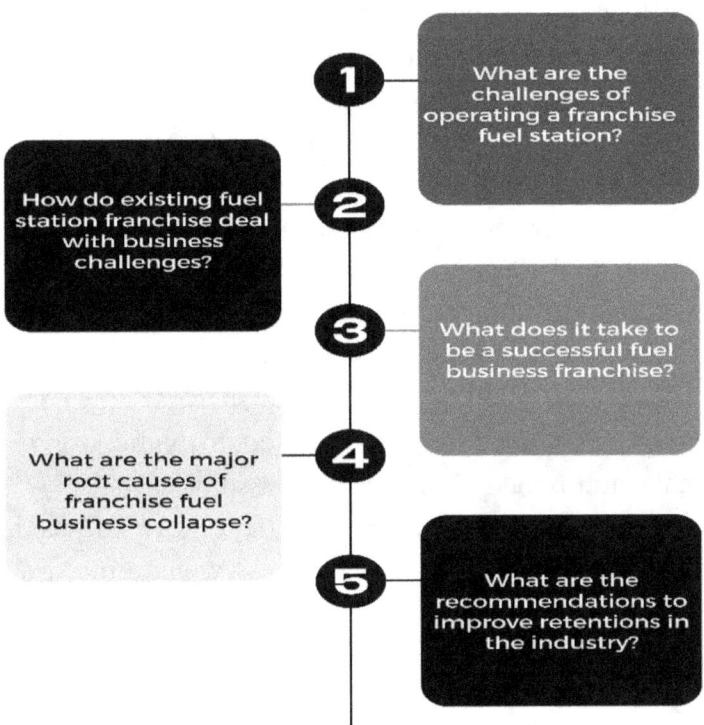

1. What are the challenges of operating a franchise fuel station?
2. How do existing fuel station franchise deal with business challenges?
3. What does it take to be a successful fuel business franchise?
4. What are the major root causes of franchise fuel business collapse?
5. What are the recommendations to improve retentions in the industry?

1.7 Significance of the research

The fuel industry is a regulated industry (SAPIA: 2008: 15). Retail pump prices are adjusted by the government. This means that players in the industry are not at liberty to determine the prices. Furthermore, the margin both for the oil company and the dealer are fixed by the government. It is perceived that the rate of increase of the cost of doing business is not at the rate at which government revises the fixed margin. An increase in pump prices does not necessary mean the margin has been increased by the government.

Every year hundreds of existing petrol stations in South Africa and elsewhere are listed for sale or lease. Oil companies frequently repossess petrol stations leading to loss of staggering amount of investment and pound of the flesh put in by the dealer. There are reports of stations closing down leading to job losses and a knock on effect on the GDP. Studies which have been conducted before have not substantively dealt with the root causes of the above. There are inadequate publications which potential dealers and other stakeholders can rely on before taking the plunge into the sector. The study investigated a wide range of detailed challenges that contribute to petrol station collapse including what makes successful dealers to be successful. The study has contributed to highlighting issues that make and break retail fuel business investors.

The government as a regulator will gain more knowledge on how to protect the fuel retail business which employs more than 50,000 pump attendants country wide. Additionally, oil companies will also see where they could be failing and not giving more as a franchisor.

Due to lack of adequate information about investing in retail business, most potential investors take the plunge without adequate due diligence and fore knowledge of the challenges of operating a fuel station. After business commencement, they soon discover that it is a totally different world from the one they thought it would be. Because of this reality, the outcome of the research has added value to the domain of the much needed investment information for decision making.

CHAPTER 2:

2.1 Introduction

Secondary information from various stakeholders concerning retail fuel business both from South Africa and abroad was examined. There seems to be a similar pattern of variables affecting fuel dealers in many countries. One of the challenges is that there is little information about the topic under study. Therefore, many investors enter the retail fuel business without adequate due diligence.

This review covers franchise fuel business, challenges of operating a franchise fuel business, shortcomings of operating a franchise fuel station and causes of fuel business collapse to mention but a fuel. What is franchising? According to Spinelli, Rosenberg and Birley (2004:2), franchising happens when someone develops a business model and sells the rights to operate it to another entrepreneur, a franchisee. Wikipedia defines franchising as the practice of using another firm's successful business model.

2.2 Problems of owning a franchise

The simplest way to understand what a franchise is to think of the most famous franchise in the world; McDonalds. Many people from all across the world have dreams of owning and operating a famous franchise like McDonalds. But is owning a franchise or a traditional store front business really worth it? Would owning a business really bring about happiness?

The first problem is money. Most franchises require a huge

capital outlay. Cooper (2012:1) reports that a franchisee needs a minimum net of USD 1 million to be placed on a list to attend Hamburger University in Chicago, Illinois. This is the university every McDonalds business owner must attend to learn how to successfully manage their store in the United States of America (USA).

The second problem of owning a franchisee is that it is actually very risky. Approximately 70-80% of traditional store front businesses fail within the first 2-5 years. And the percentages are getting worse as the economy suffers. In addition, the average "successful" business usually does not start consistently turning in a profit for some time.

The third problem of owning a franchise is the long hours required to work day in and day out. This calls for a lot of endurance and hard work on the part of the franchisee. The average business owner works 15-18 hours a day managing their business. It is too hard for too little (Cooper, 2012:1) in many cases.

The fourth problem is franchisee fees. The franchise fees can be a real pain. They cut into the small margins that accrue to franchisees on top of paying for other operational costs. Paying franchisee fees or royalties is the order of the day in the franchisee industry. What is even more challenging is that more often than not, fees are paid as a percentage of the turnover and not on the franchisee gross profit.

2.3 Franchised fuel business

Fuel business is subdivided into upstream business and downstream business. Upstream business consists of all fuel related activities from exploration to the refinery. Downstream business consists of fuel related activities from the refinery to the consumers. oil companies and refineries fall in the wholesale segment. To bring fuel business closer to consumers, oil companies build petrol stations and look for dealers to operate the stations under a dealership agreement. The dealer is called a franchisee (Chinambu, 2011:24). In some cases, the oil companies partially or entirely operate the retail network. Petrol stations operations on 24 hours basis.

The franchisee is expected to pay franchisee fees on top of paying the operational costs of running the station. In addition, the franchisee has to buy fuel from the franchisor only. To be selected as a franchisee, the prospect must meet stringent requirements including evidence of financial acumen. According to Cyrus Business Brokers (2012:1), petrol stations sell in the range of 2.3 million South African Rands for small stations to as high as 20 million South African Rands for big stations. The capital requirement to buy or rent a petrol station varies considerably from country to country. In addition, some brands are more expensive than others.

Alternatively, any individual can build a station and then approach any oil company for branding. In such an arrangement, the oil company will pay rentals to the one who built it. The one who built it may apply to be given priority to operate the station if interested. If not interested, the oil company will find a dealer elsewhere. Fuel franchising is therefore, a business arrangement where the oil company grants certain rights to an agent or dealer or franchisee to operate under the principal's business brand name in line with an established system of doing business.

2.4 The challenges of operating a franchise fuel business

The study investigated the challenges of owning a franchise

fuel business in the Republic of South Africa. Franchise fuel business constitutes what is known as the retail fuel business. All petrol stations also called service stations fall in this category. They service motorists. It is now a common phenomenon to regard a retail site as a convenience centre because the site constitutes a convenience shop, coffee bar, toilets, car wash facilities among other services in most cases.

As highlighted by Cyrus Business Brokers (2012:1), to buy or lease a petrol station requires considerable amount of capital for an ordinary person. Thankfully, this burden is mitigated by franchise financing to some extent. It is easier to get a bank loan to fund a proven franchise system than an unproven business system. Cyrus Business Brokers have reported on their website that for an oil company to approve a deal, an investor must have at least 50% of the capital as own money. This is still a challenge for an average person.

According to the Department of Energy of the Republic of South Africa (2012:1), petrol and diesel prices in South Africa are linked to the price of crude oil in international markets which is quoted in US dollars (US $) per barrel (a barrel is approximately equal to 159 litres). International crude oil prices are susceptible to the law of demand and supply. Crude oil prices combined with the Rand/Dollar exchange rate have a major impact on fuel prices. This forex risk exposure.

To this end, oil companies and their franchisees are required to deal with factors (crude oil price and exchange rate) that are beyond their control. They must brace themselves for fluctuating gas prices, inflating overhead costs and safety aspects. These factors increase the working capital requirements.

In addition, dealer margins are determined by the Department of Energy. Traders such as Shell, Caltex, Sasol, BP and Engen among others cannot increase their regulated tariffs or alter their license conditions without regulatory approval. While in some countries, regulation is light handed, there is heavy politically charged regulation in some countries.

The potential for perpetual labour disputes from refinery workers and transporters is another challenge. These challenges make the sector volatile and could lead to a high dealer turnover and business collapse.

It is not easy to operate in this sector. A franchisee cannot determine own margins. The sector is fraught with high risks such as high flammability of products leading to high insurance costs and exposure to criminals due to high cash build up on the stations. In addition, investing in the industry requires high capital outlay. As though this is not enough, dealer margins are thin and only revised at the discretion of the regulator. Thin margins are on all continents. To this end, petrol stations have been transforming to convenience centres as per given example below.

On 17th June, 2011, John Dulgaro; Caltex Retail Operations Manager-Australia said the following, "over the past 20 years, we have transformed our business from service stations to convenience stores. In the process, Caltex has become one of Australia's biggest franchisors, with over 85% of our retail network operated by independent franchisees." This statement showed a changing pattern from concentrating on fuel business to including several services on one site.

Challenges in this industry abound. First and foremost, it is a regulated industry. You cannot just wake up and decide to increase pump prices. Pump prices are announced by the government through the Department of Energy or a regulator in almost all countries of the world.

In addition, a petrol station runs like an airport or a hospital. It is expected to operate nonstop. This leads to increased overhead costs and consistent exposure to a high risk of attacks from criminals and theft by employees. Dealers must remain at the business premises most of the time for extended hours leading to stress.

2.5 Causes of fuel business collapse

Because of the perceived lucrative business opportunity offered by fuel business, many people dream of owning a famous fuel station. The prestige and other trophies of life that appear to accompany many petrol franchise owners leaves the wider uninformed society bewildered and entrenched in the feeling that fuel business is indeed the popular "black gold;" an escape into the secluded wealthy class and a terminator of financial squalor and hopelessness. It appears that prospective franchisees do not pay adequate attention to the crucial six step franchise investigation process, (Mathews, Debolt, and Percival, 2011:185). The end result of not following the process can be tragic.

The retail sector operates in a highly competitive environment that is characterised by thin profit margins and a high stock turn over. It is both capital and labour intensive with at least 58,000 pump attendants employed in the sector (Thomas, 2005:45). According to a 2004 study conducted by the Department of Minerals and Energy (DME), the average fuel station sold 270,000 litres per month with approximately 70% of all fuel stations selling only 200,000 (Thomas, 2005:45). Despite the regulation in the industry, the DME found that only 40% of fuel stations are profitable with regard to selling fuel. Therefore, those petrol stations without adequate non-fuel business are likely to suffer.

A survey conducted on 74 BP sites around South Africa

revealed that 66% of people visiting the fuel station did so with the main purpose of buying from the convenience store. In comparison, only 34% visited the service station to purchase fuel (Peacock Consulting, 2004). Therefore, including extra facilities on a retail site is a matter of survival and not a luxury. Other additional services include banking and ATM, car wash, fast food outlets, motor car sales, lotto outlets, public telephones and cellular telephone suppliers (Human Sciences Research Council, 1992:32)

To show how this problem is geographically extended, the Seattle Times in the United States of America quoted convenience store owner, David Malik who owns seven gas stations in South King County. According to Malik, he earned as much on a can of coke as he does on a typical 10 gallon purchase of gas. He further stated that every time the price of gas went up, it cost them (dealers) more money. A retailer's margin on a gallon of gas is very small and most rely on in-store sales of beverages and cigarettes to make money (Seattle Times, 2006:1). The challenge appears to hinge on the fact that margins are fixed and revised by government. To try and relieve the financial burden on dealers, suggestions have stated that oil companies reduce the excessive high rentals they demand for their sides (FleetCube, 2005:1).

Many fuel stations have explored alternative sources of income in order to remain profitable and there is a concern that there are too many fuel stations resulting in an over traded market (Thomas, 2005: 46). According to the DME, the retail market may be overtraded by as much as 30% (Visser, 2005). Probably, this is one of the reasons the Fuel Retailers Association (FRA) has been instrumental in opposing new service station proliferations by using framework within the Petroleum Products Acts in order to ensure survival of existing retailers (Forecourt Times, 2010:5). The FRA main objective is observe, consult and negotiate on an industry basis on any issue relevant to the well being and enhancement of fuel retailers.

Disregarding the dealership provisions leads to the termination of the franchise business. Because fuel business is high cash turnover business, the potential for cash accumulation on the site leading to a high risk profile. Poor risk management can lead to business collapse. Fuel business is a tough business with extended working hours round the clock. To survive the dealer must have strong passion for the business, strong financial management skills and strong leadership skills just to mention a few.

K. Sartorius, C Eitzen and J. Hart (researchers) from the University of Witwatersrand, Johannesburg, South Africa conducted a relatively detailed examination of the variables influencing the fuel retail industry. Their study focussed on analysing the impact of location of the petrol station, size of the petrol station and fuel price on the profitability of the site. The results were quite interesting. The location of any retail business is an important factor affecting the performance of that business (Chan, Padmanabhan and Seetharaman, 2005:10). Their study revealed that the demand for petrol can be expressly linked to local geographical and demographic factors such as population, median income, number of cars, proximity to airport, downtown and high ways.

To this end, rural population could be considered less profitable compared to urban ones. A review of rural petrol stations in Scotland indicated that to be viable, these stations should be more than 8 miles to the next petrol station or more than 30 minutes' drive from the edge of a town with a population of 30,000 or more (Scottish Executive Publications, 2006:1).

Therefore, it can be argued that there is a correlation between location and potential profitability.

The study revealed that another important location factor that could affect fuel demand is the accessibility of the site to customers (Lee and Schmidt, 1980:55-65). Street intersection sites and corner sites are preferred locations as they offer better access, improved visibility, and higher traffic volume and a signalised intersection improves access into and out of the fuel station (Smalley, 1999: 339-347).

It is a known fact that the size of the petrol station and the number of pumping bays available is an indication of the convenience of filling at a particular station. Customer convenience is an important variable that has a significant influence on sales volume. Additionally, the price factor has been identified as one of the key variables affecting the demand of fuel (Graham and Glaister, 2002: 1-26).

Although, the above study correctly identified and proved that the location, size of the station and the price do impact the profitability of the site, it is a concern that it did not exert as much emphasis on other key metrics that impact on the station. The price may be acceptable but if the margin which is fixed by a third party (government) remains small and inadequate to cover rising costs of doing business, a dealer can lose his working capital.

No matter how big the petrol station is, with a good location, if product quality is not guaranteed, a dealer can lose business. No matter how good the three focus areas in the study could be, if the dealer has financial indiscipline, he will lose his investment. He can also lose his business if there is inadequate support from the oil company (franchiser) such as timely repair works on malfunctioning pumps, branding and lack of favourable trade terms among other issues.

Without casting aspersions on the above study it was felt that it fell short of presenting a broad spectrum that impact on profitability. Even in Nigeria where pump prices are so low (less than USD 0.5 a litre while RSA pump prices are more than USD 1 per litre and Nigeria's population is over 160 million while RSA is 49 million), dealers have still lost their investments.

On 1 st January, 2010, The Daily Trust, an online Nigerian publication carried a headline story titled: "Nigeria- country's sea of empty petrol stations." The article carried the following statement: "Many are worried at the large and increasing number of petrol stations in the country that are not functioning or functioning under par and are calling on the relevant authorities to either sanction or close such stations, as they constitute a nuisance and needless frustration to motorists. A respondent Sina Ayodele was particularly unhappy at the presence of such filling stations along the nation's highways, while crisscrossing the expanse of the nation (Daily Trust, 2010:1).

In some cases, it appears dealers lose working capital and have challenges accessing financing. Learning how to protect one's investment is extremely important. It is important to understand and learn how banks differentiate good franchises from the bad (Lambert, September 2011, 1).

When one analyses the pattern, several questions remain unanswered. Probably the authors of "Franchising 101: The complete Guide to Evaluating, Buying and Growing your Franchise Business," were correct when they said, "Purchasing a franchise is a major life decision that requires careful deliberation. Unfortunately, many people spend more time investigating the selection of a penny stock than they do investigating a franchise opportunity; even though a franchise will tie up enormous assets for many, many years-" The

Association of Small Business Development Centres (1998:1). The editor of the "Your Business Magazine April/May 2012: 2) emphasises that the long term success of business relies on one's ability to plan and prepare for the challenges and opportunities that come one's way.

Hence this study focussed on a broad range of factors in order to try and present a major schedule or matrix of factors that form part of a web of challenges of owning a petrol station. This study reviews how existing dealers deal with their day to day major challenges. In addition, it reveals what successful dealers focus on as a priority. According to Taylor (2008: 1), some of the common mistakes gas station investors make include under or over estimating forecasted financials, choosing a poor location, lack of operational experience and under capitalisation.

As correctly observed by Hewitt (2012: 1), gas station business is extraordinarily competitive. Business owners that select an excellent location and run an inviting convenience store, car wash or auto mechanic shop can turn a steady profit. As with any business, gas stations have some complexities including environmental issues related to gasoline storage that make it challenging. In addition profit margins on gasoline can be less than 10 %, making it important to develop alternative revenue streams.

Dealing with challenges in the retail fuel sector

Molefe (2006: ii) reported that the forecourt convenience shops are not price regulated and hence have become a strategic revenue generator for petrol station operators. This is one of the strategies being used to help maximise earnings from a petrol station. It is virtually impossible to build a modern petrol station without incorporating in adequate non fuel related business.

Furthermore, there is an emerging strong advocacy by industry bodies such as the Fuel Retailers Association (FRA). The primary objective of the FRA is to promote and protect the best interests of Fuel Retailers and its members in particular. It is a financially and fully autonomous association that ensures the survival and success for its members who are fuel service station owners in the retailing of fuel in South Africa (Forecourt Times, 2012:2)

Although the high capital requirement is an entry barrier into the sector, it is also a strategic requirement by franchisors to ensure that only financially capable investors operate in the sector. It is believed that meeting such a requirement would minimise business failure due to inadequate working capital.

In order to minimise the impact of stock outs in petrol stations due to transportation challenges, most leading oil companies have their own dedicated delivery trucks. This strategy has worked well especially in times of striking workers in the transport sector. The bulk of fuel is transported by contracted transporters.

Every business is exposed to risk. It is worse for the fuel industry. The fuel price is linked to the crude oil price which is not produced in South Africa. This means that fuel dealers are exposed to price escalations due to market forces beyond their control. The volatile exchange rate also compounds the situation. The potential for fraud and criminal attacks is high in petrol stations due to high cash turnover.

To counter these challenges, any sensible dealer is expected to procure insurance packages across the business. A dealer can procure an insurance fuel guarantee as an alternative to a bank guarantee allowing for the release of tied-up capital.

This is typical in cases where an oil company has requested a candidate dealer to provide cash/ bank guarantee before the deal is signed. The guarantee is not part of the huge working capital. It is similar to putting up a security deposit in the rental business.

2.6 Conclusion

There are many factors that lead to the success and failure of many franchise fuel businesses. The understanding of these factors is critical to the survival of this type of business. Franchise fuel business is unique in that the margins are regulated and adjusted by government unlike other franchises. Due to political pressure, it is unlikely that government grant robust fuel margins. It is has emerged from the above review that non fuel business on a retail site has the potential to bring in more net profits than fuel business.

CHAPTER 3:

3.1 Target Population for the research

The target population for this study consisted of fuel retailers in the Gauteng Province of the Republic of South Africa. Fuel retailers market fuel on behalf their principals. The principals include Engen, BP, Shell, Sasol, Total and Caltex. As of 2002, the Gauteng Province had 1,582 retailers out of 5,112 countrywide representing 31 % of the total petrol stations (Matsho, 2002:2).

However, latest information according to the South African Petroleum Industry Association (SAPIA) indicated that there are approximately 4,600 petrol stations throughout the country (SAPIA, 2012:1). The petrol station population has declined. Therefore the population of the petrol stations in the Gauteng may be adjusted by 31% leading to a target population of approximately 1,426 for the purpose of this study.

3.2 The research instrument which was used to conduct the research

There are several ways of collecting data during a research. Data can be collected through interviews or questionnaires, depending on the research paradigm being employed. In this study, data was collected using a questionnaire as a research instrument.

Evaluate the adequacy of the data for the research questions.

3.3 Data analysis of the research

Data was coded and captured in Microsoft Excel. Thereafter, it was exported to IBM Statistical Package for the Social Sciences 19 (SPSS computer program) for analysis. In order to make scientific conclusions, it was ensured that tests of statistical significance such as the Chi Square and gamma were used. These tests were preferred due to the ordinal nature of data collected. Furthermore, normality tests, factor analysis, Kruskal Wallis test and Spearman's Rho (9) correlations were done (McClave Benson Sincich, 2008:29).

Chi Square tested the association between two variables. This assisted in arriving at credible conclusion otherwise there would be no basis to generalise an association for instance between location of business and dealer business success throughout the population. Factor analysis to see which factors best accounted for the variability in the collected data was used. It was important to find out if factors such as those responsible for business collapse could be generalised throughout the population. To help achieve this outcome, detailed statistical analysis was conducted.

3.4 Ensuring validity and reliability

From a statistical point of view, the Cronbach's alpha was calculated. The Cronbach's alpha is a coefficient of reliability used to gauge the internal consistency or reliability of data in a given sample. Reliability testing is one of the pillars of inferential statistical problems (McClave Benson Sincich, 2008:10).

In addition, the research questions were relevant to the plight of the dealers because they sought to address some of their nagging concerns. As such, there was a high likelihood that participants would cooperate and give answers as relating to their situations.

CHAPTER 4:

STATEMENT OF RESULTS, DISCUSSION AND INTERPRETATION

4.1 Introduction

This chapter focuses on the research findings, discussion and linking to literature review. These findings are presented graphically and statistically. They are presented and read in conjunction with the research objectives. Statistical analysis was done using IBM SPSS 19.

Sample characteristics

Out of the targeted 170 franchisees, 150 franchisees participated in the research. Therefore, these findings are derived from 150 participants from the Gauteng Province. The response rate was 88 % of the targeted sample size during the allocated survey period.

The sample was homogeneous from an operational point of view. This was due to the fact that the sector sells the same commodity and is regulated by government. There are stringent licensing conditions. Adherence to these license conditions potentially creates a level ground and homogeneous sector. All dealers operate under a similar license from the Department of Energy. For homogenous populations, sample sizes do not necessarily ought to be robust (Israel, 2012:1).

As of 2002, the Gauteng Province had 1,582 retailers out of 5,112 countrywide representing 31 % of the total petrol stations (Matsho, 2002:2). However, latest information according to the South African Petroleum Industry Association (SAPIA) indicated that there were approximately 4,600 petrol stations throughout the country (SAPIA, 2012:1). The petrol station population has declined by 31%. Therefore, the population of the petrol stations in the Gauteng was adjusted by 31% leading to a target population of approximately 1,426 for the purpose of this study. 150 participants represent approximately 10.5% of the population.

Demographic profile of franchisees

Part of the purpose of the research was to capture the demographic profile of the participants covering gender, years of experience in retail fuel business and number of dealers before the incumbent. The following is the outcome:

Table 4.1: Gender distribution

	Frequency	Percent	Valid Percent	Cumulative Percent
Male	123	82.0	82.0	82.0
Female	27	18.0	18.0	100
Total	150	100	100	

According to Table 4.1, 82% of participants are male, and 18%

are female (N = 150).

Figure 4.1: Gender distribution

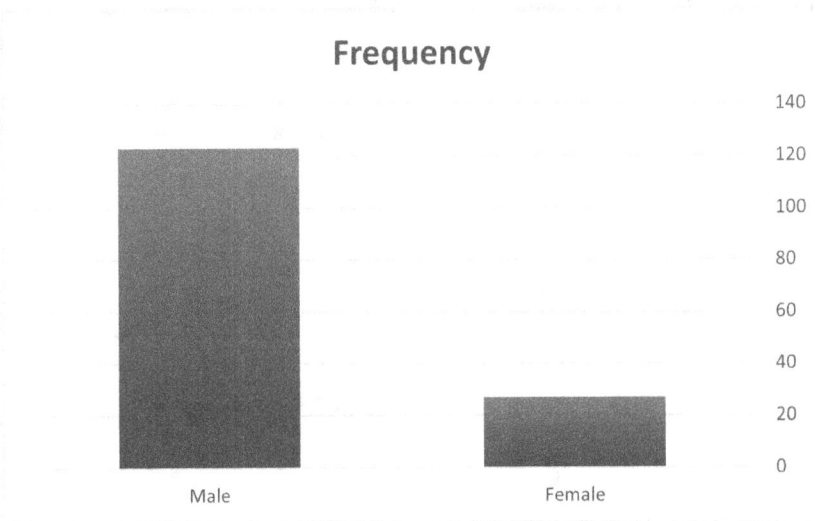

Table 4.2: Years of experience in retail fuel business

	Frequency	Percent	Valid Percent	Cumulative Percent
0-1	19	12.7	12.9	12.9
2-5	29	19.3	19.7	32.7
6-10	43	28.7	29.3	61.9
> 10	56	37.3	38.1	100
Total	147	98.0	100.0	100.0
Missing System	3	2.0		
Total	150	100		

According to Table 4.2, 12.9% of participants had between 0-1 years' experience, 19.7% between 2 – 5 years, 29.3% between

6 – 10 years, and 38.1% over 10 years (N = 147)

This outcome confirmed the high rate of dealer turnover reported in the literature review. The sector does not have many long term investors and stations appear to be exchanging hands regularly.

Figure 4.2: Years of experience in retail fuel business

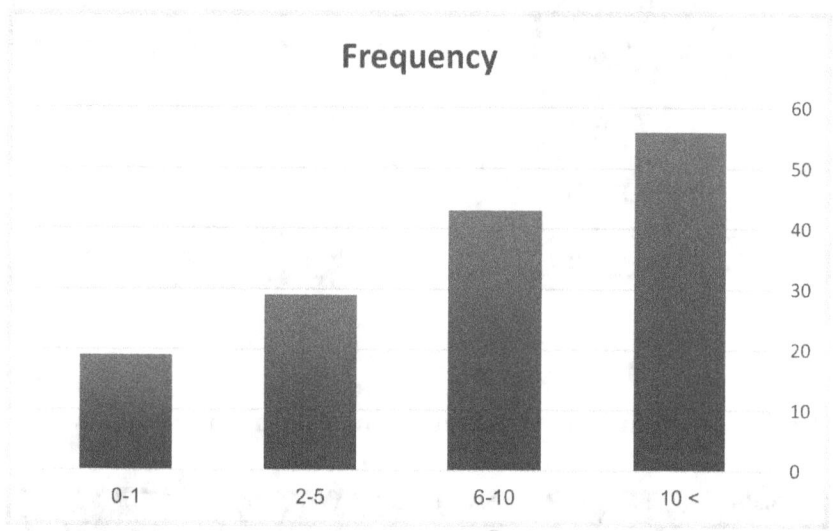

Table 4.3: Number of previous dealers before the incumbent

	Frequency	Percent	Valid Percent	Cumulative Percent
0–1	33	22.0	24.1	24.1
2–5	56	37.3	40.9	65.0
6–10	37	24.7	27.0	92.0
> 10	11	7.3	8.0	100
Total	137	91.3	100.0	
Missing System	13	8.7		
Total	150	100		

According to Table 4.3, 24.1% of participants reported between 0 – 1 previous dealers, 40.9% between 2 – 5, 27% between 6 – 10, and 8% over 10 (N = 137).

There was a positive correlation between number of previous dealers and profitability margin (r = 0.248, N =137). Frequent dealer turnover could in part be due to small size of profit margins. The majority of the participants own petrol stations which have been owned before. This confirms the high dealer turnover reported in the first paragraph of page 10 under literature review in this study.

Figure 4.3: Number of previous dealers before the incumbent

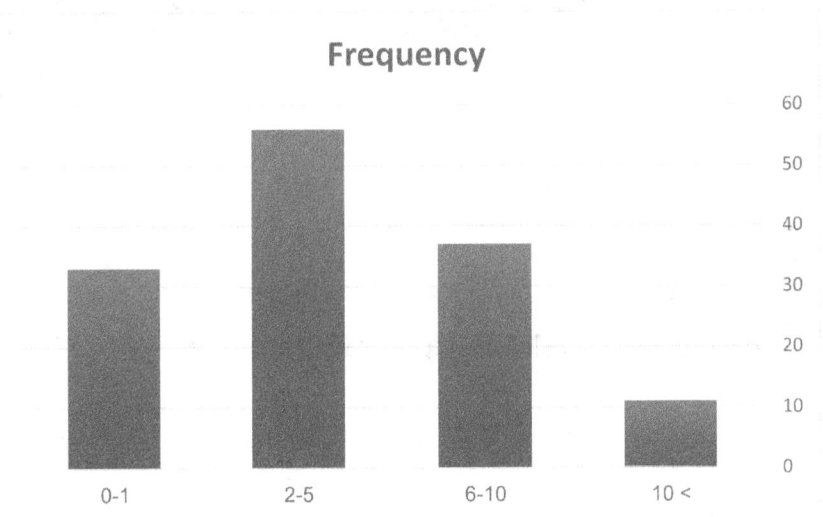

Section B of the research

Section B of the research question dealt with challenges of operating in the retail fuel business. The research question was as follows:

What are the challenges of operating a franchise fuel business?

Participants considered five challenges under this question. Each challenge is listed on top of a frequency table.

Table 4.4: Challenge of dealer margin adjustment

I cannot determine my own dealer margin

	Frequency	Percent	Valid Percent	Cumulative Percent
Strongly Disagree	9	6.0	6.0	6.0
Disagree	19	12.7	12.7	18.7
Neutral	13	8.7	8.7	27.3
Agree	69	46.0	46.0	73.3
Strongly Agree	40	26.7	26.7	100.0
Total	150	100	100	

According to Table 4.4 1a, 6% of participants strongly disagreed, 12.7% disagreed, 8.7% were neutral, 46% agree, and 26.7% strongly agreed that one of the challenges of operating a franchise fuel station was that dealers could not determine their own dealer margin (N = 150).

Additionally, a slight positive correlation ($r = 0.097$, $N = 150$) between inability to determine own margins and risky nature of business was observed. The correlation was not strong since heavy price regulation was on petrol. There was no government price regulation on diesel in South Africa at the time of the research.

Figure 4.4: Challenge of dealer margin determination

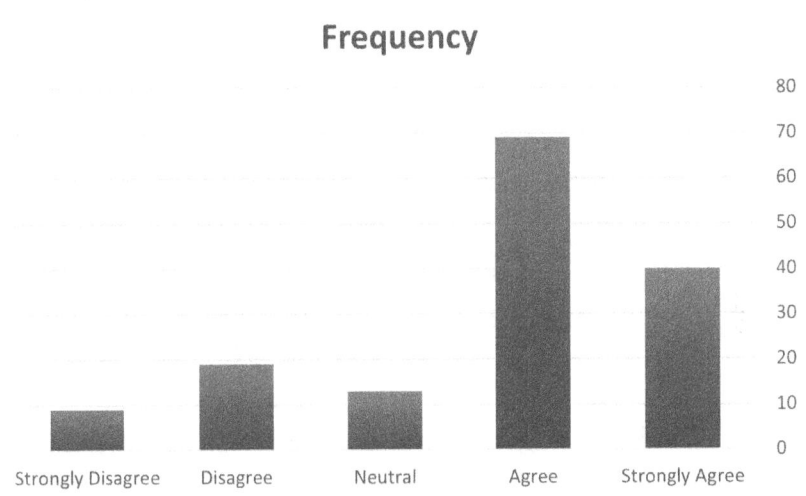

Table 4.5: Challenge of business risk

It is high risk business

	Frequency	Percent	Valid Percent	Cumulative Percent
Strongly Disagree	3	2.0	2.0	2.0
Disagree	12	8.0	8.0	10.0
Neutral	16	10.7	10.7	20.7
Agree	84	56.0	56.0	76.7
Strongly Agree	35	23.3	23.3	100.0
Total	150	100.0	100.0	

According to Table 4.5, 1b, 2% of participants strongly disagreed, 8% disagreed, 10.7% were neutral, 56.0% agreed and 23.3% strongly agreed that one of the challenges of operating a franchise fuel station was that it is a high-risk business (N = 150).

There was a very low correlation between perception that retail fuel business is high risk business and gender. This means that the risky nature of this business has nothing to do with gender. Both male and female perceive the sector as a risk sector. During literature review stage, it was established that petrol stations are high risk areas. It is not only about huge sums of cash that can be found at petrol stations but fuel is also an inflammable substance (page 8)

Figure 4.5: Challenge of business risk

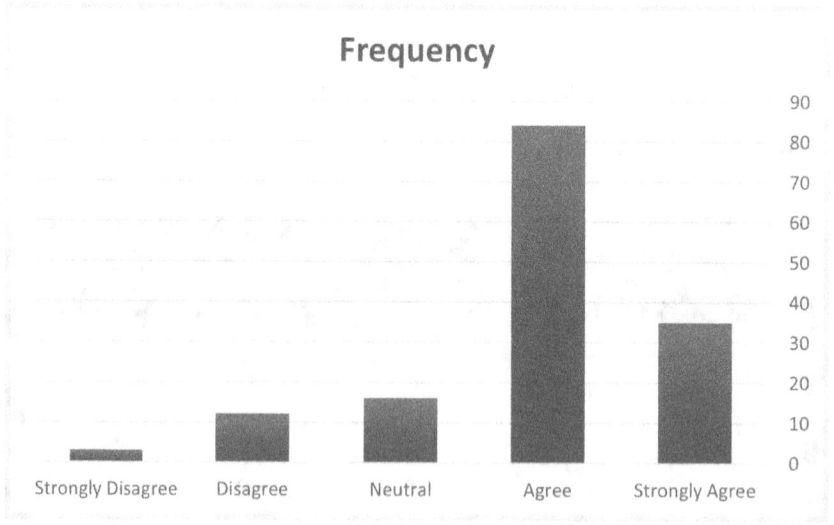

Table 4.6: Challenge of high capital requirement

High capital requirements

	Frequency	Percent	Valid Percent	Cumulative Percent
Strongly Disagree	3	2.0	2.0	2.0
Disagree	7	4.7	4.7	6.7
Neutral	24	16.0	16.0	22.7
Agree	84	56.0	56.0	78.7
Strongly Agree	32	21.3	21.3	100.0
Total	150	100	100	

According to Table 4.6, 1c, 2% of participants strongly disagreed, 4.7% disagreed, 16% were neutral, 56% agree, and 21.3% strongly agreed that one of the challenges of operating a franchise fuel station was high capital requirements (N = 150).

There is a moderate correlation ($r = 0.262$, N=150) between high capital requirements and risk management skills. Naturally, a high capital business calls for good risk management skills. This confirms findings at literature review stage that petrol stations are constantly exposed to risks of being attacked by bandits and high capital requirements.

Figure 4.6: Challenge of high capital requirement

High capital requirements

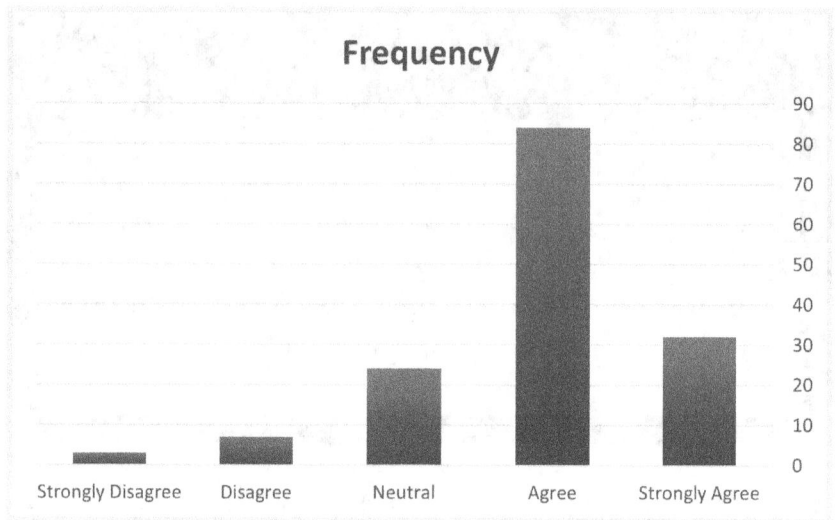

Table 4.7: Challenge of profit margin size

Profit Margin is very thin

	Frequency	Percent	Valid Percent	Cumulative Percent
Disagree	15	10.0	10.0	10.0
Neutral	24	16.0	16.0	26.0
Agree	59	39.3	39.3	65.3
Strongly Agree	52	34.7	34.7	100.0
Total	150	100	100	

According to Table 4.7, 1d, 10% of participants disagreed, 16% were neutral, 39.3% agreed, 34.7% strongly agreed that one of the challenges of operating a franchise fuel station was that the profit margin was very thin (N = 150).

There was a positive correlation in terms of challenges in operating a franchise fuel station attributable to the profit margin being very small, and that business depends on location (r = 0.471, N = 150). This means that the more likely the identified shortcoming is that the location is bad, the more likely the profit margin will be small. Even under literature review, location emerged as a critical business driver (page 12).

Figure 4.7: Challenge of profit margin size

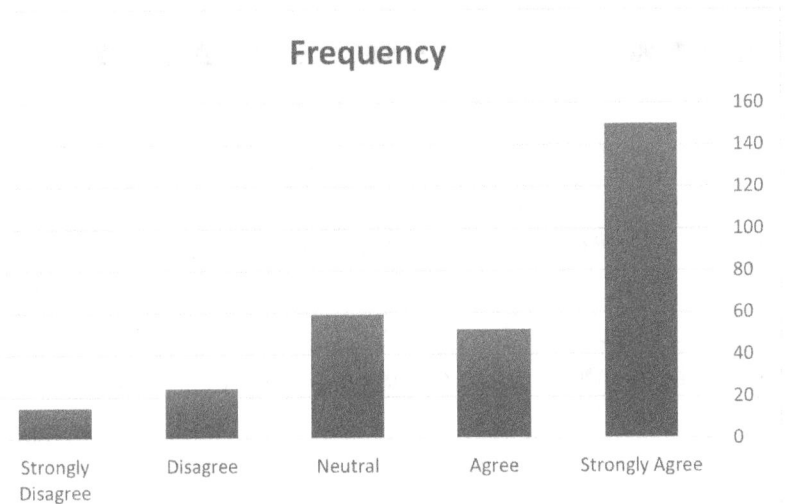

Table 4.8: Challenge of business location

Business depends on location

	Frequency	Percent	Valid Percent	Cumulative Percent
Strongly Disagree	1	7	7	7
Disagree	3	2.0	2.0	2.7
Neutral	10	6.7	6.7	9.3
Agree	69	46.0	46.0	55.3
Strongly Agree	67	44.7	44.7	100.0
Total	150	100	100	

According to Table 4.8, 1e, 0.7% of participants strongly disagreed, 2% disagreed, 6.7% were neutral, 46% agreed, and 44.7% strongly agreed that one of the challenges of operating a franchise fuel station was that business depended on location (N = 150). There was a fair correlation between profit margin and business location ($r = 0.471$, N=150). It would appear that the better the location, the more likely is the profit and vice versa.

Figure 4.8: Challenge of business location

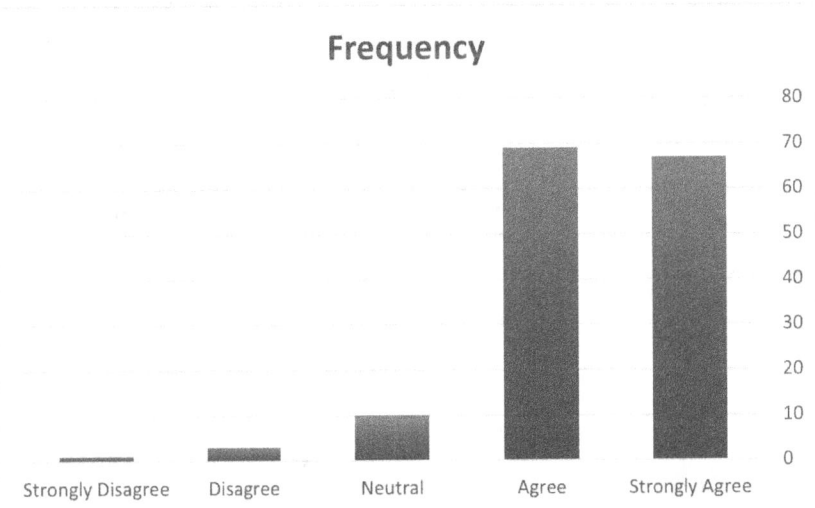

Table 4.9: Electronic fuel management system availability

I have an electronic fuel management system in place

	Frequency	Percent	Valid Percent	Cumulative Percent
Strongly Disagree	1	7	7	7
Disagree	4	2.7	2.7	3.3
Neutral	30	20.0	20.0	23.3
Agree	70	46.7	46.7	70.0
Strongly Agree	45	30	30	100.0
Total	150	100	100	

According to Table 4.9, 2b, 0.7% of participants strongly disagreed, 2.7% disagreed, 20% were neutral, 46.7% agreed, and 30% strongly agreed that one of the ways in which existing fuel franchises can deal with challenges is by having an electronic fuel management system in place (N = 150). A fuel management system is a critical integrated software that monitors product movement in the tanks and sales. It helps with managing re-order levels.

Figure 4.9: Electronic management system availability

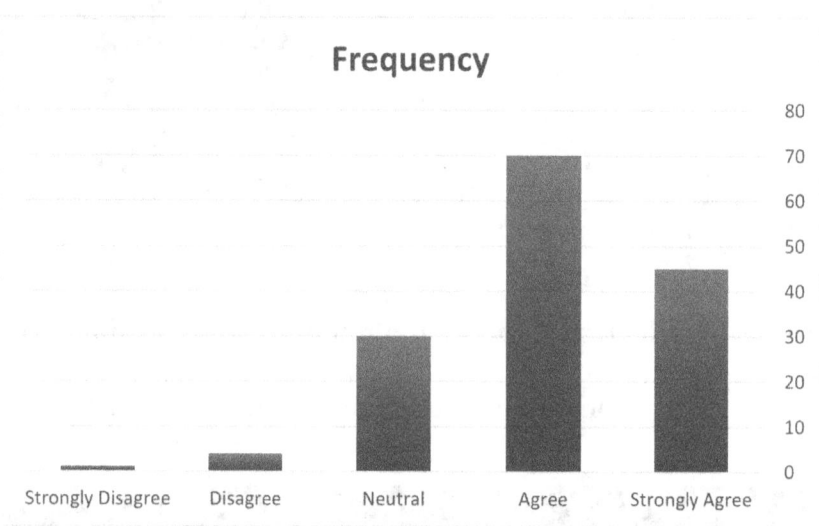

Table 4.10: Degree of dealer financial discipline

	Frequency	Percent	Valid Percent	Cumulative Percent
Disagree	1	7	7	7
Neutral	22	14.7	14.7	15.3
Agree	88	58.7	58.7	74.0
Strongly Agree	39	26.0	26.0	100.0
Total	150	100	100	

According to Table 4.10, 0.7% of participants disagreed, 14.7% were neutral, 58.7% agreed, and 26% strongly agreed that one of the ways in which existing fuel franchises can deal with challenges is by having a strong financial discipline (N = 150). There is a positive correlation (r =0.2, N=150) between strong financial discipline and profit margin being very small. It appears that the size of the profit margin encourages strong financial discipline.

Figure 4.10: Degree of dealer financial discipline

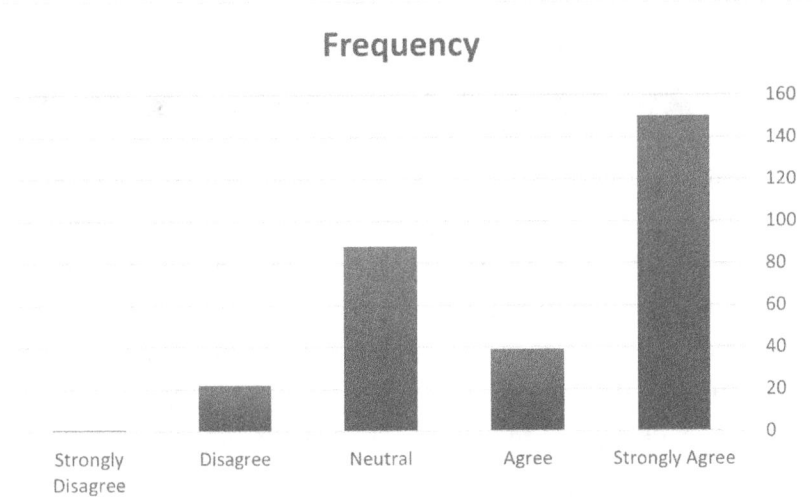

Table 4.11: Focus on building profitability

I am focused on building profitability

	Frequency	Percent	Valid Percent	Cumulative Percent
Disagree	5	3.3	3.3	3.3
Neutral	14	9.3	9.3	12.7
Agree	73	48.7	48.7	61.3
Strongly Agree	58	38.7	38.7	100.0
Total	150	100	100	

According to Table 4.11, 2a, 3.3% of participants disagreed, 9.3% were neutral, 48.7% agreed, and 38.7% strongly agreed that one of the ways in which existing fuel franchisees can deal with challenges is by focusing on building profitability (N = 150). There is a significant association between the number of years of experience in the business and the manners in which challenges are dealt with by dealers in terms of focusing on business profitability (Pr = 34.233, n = 147, p 0.0001).

Figure 4.11: Focus on building profitability

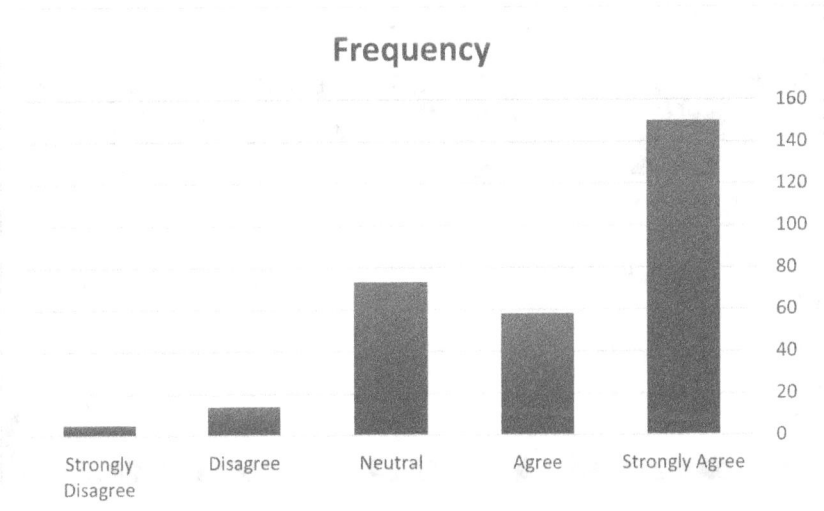

According to Table 4.11, 3.3% of respondents disagreed, 9.3% were neutral, 48.7% agreed, and 38.7% strongly agreed that one of the ways in which existing fuel franchises and dealers can deal with challenges is by focusing on building profitability (N = 150). There is a significant association between the number of years of experience in the business and the manners in which challenges are dealt with by dealers in terms of focusing on business profitability (Pr = 34.233, n = 147, p 0.0001).

Table 4.12: Insurance adequacy

I have adequate insurance cover

	Frequency	Percent	Valid Percent	Cumulative Percent
Strongly Disagree	2	1.3	1.3	1.3
Disagree	4	2.7	2.7	4.0
Neutral	24	16.0	16.0	20.0
Agree	92	61.3	61.3	81.3
Strongly Agree	28	18.7	18.7	100.0
Total	150	100	100	

According to Table 4.12, 2d, 10.3% of participants strongly disagreed, 2.7% disagreed, 16% were neutral 61.3% agreed, and 18.7% strongly agreed that they had adequate insurance cover (N = 150).

A positive correlation ($r = 0.62$, $N = 150$) was observed between adequate insurance and high business risk. The risky nature of business spurs the need for adequate insurance.

Figure 4.12: Insurance adequacy

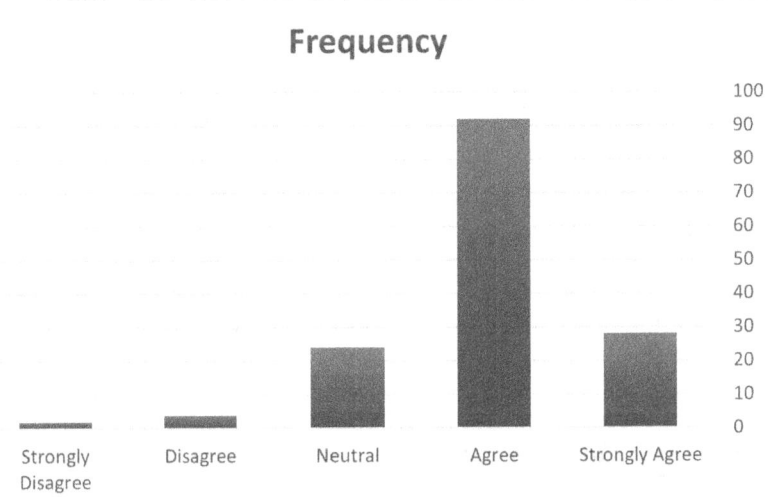

Table 4.13: Presence of non-fuel business on site

I have several other businesses on the site

	Frequency	Percent	Valid Percent	Cumulative Percent
Strongly Disagree	12	8.0	8.0	8.0
Disagree	23	15.3	15.3	23.3
Neutral	19	12.7	12.7	36.0
Agree	69	46.0	46.0	82.0
Strongly Agree	27	18.0	18.0	100.0
Total	150	100	100	

According to Table 4.13, 2e, 8% of participants strongly disagreed, 15.3% disagreed, 12.7% are neutral, 46% agreed and

18% strongly agreed that one of the ways in which existing fuel franchises and dealers could deal with challenges was by having several other businesses on site (N = 150).

A moderate correlation (r =0.2, N= 150) was observed between number of other businesses on the site and focus on building profitability. It can be concluded that developing more non fuel related business is a profit maximisation strategy.

A further positive correlation observed (r = 0.67, N= 150) between number of other businesses on the site and profit margin being small. Because the size of the fuel profit margin is very small, dealers focused on developing more non-fuel related business. This is why several petrol stations have non-fuel business incorporated into them.

Figure 4.13: Presence of non-fuel business on site

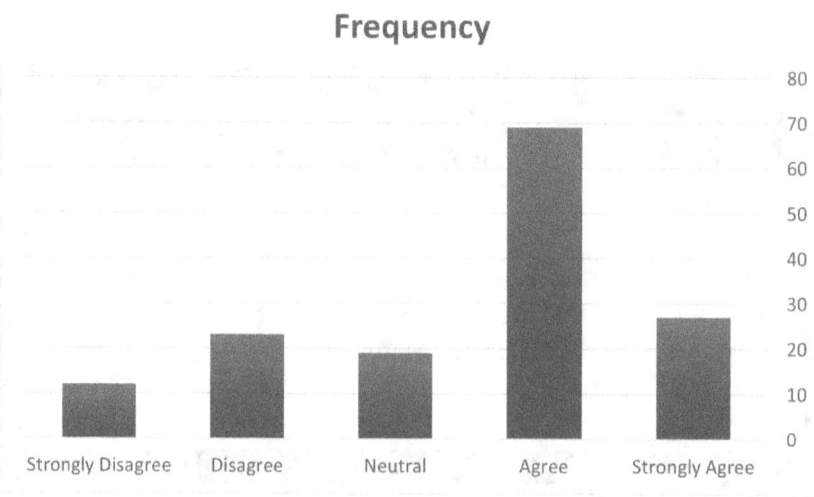

To survive in this sector, a dealer needs a very strong strategy. It is no longer enough to rely on fuel business alone on the site. For example, the majority of dealers stated that they had several other business lines on the site. This confirms what is under literature review. For example, a Caltex Retail Operations Manager-Australia reported to have said that over the last 20 years, Caltex had transformed its business from service stations to convenience stores.

Section D of the research

The purpose of this section was to investigate key success factors in retail fuel business. The research question in this section was as follows:

What does it take to be a successful fuel business dealer/ franchisee?

Participants considered five factors under this question. Each factor is listed on top of a frequency table hereunder. Listed below is how the participants rated each factor.

Table 4.14: Dealer financial management skills and business success

Strong financial management skills

	Frequency	Percent	Valid Percent	Cumulative Percent
Strongly Disagree	1	7	7	7
Disagree	2	1.3	1.3	2.0
Neutral	7	4.7	4.7	6.7
Agree	59	39.3	39.3	46.0
Strongly Agree	81	54.0	54.0	100.0
Total	150	100	100	

According to Table 4.14, 3a, 0.7% of participants strongly disagreed, 1.3% disagreed, 4.7% were neutral, 39.3% agreed, and 54% strongly agreed that a successful dealer required strong management skills (N = 150).

A positive correlation (r = 0.118, N =150) was established between the need for strong financial management skills and business risk. Furthermore, correlation tests revealed another positive correlation between strong financial management skills and size of profit margin.

Because the sector is a high risk one and the profit margins are very small, the need for strong financial discipline to overcome the challenges is a must.

Figure 4.14: Dealer financial management skills and business success

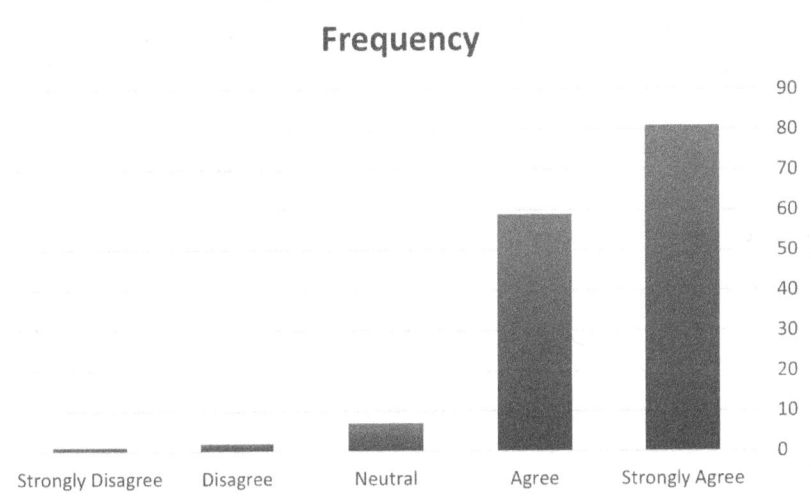

Table 4.15: Location and business success

Business location

	Frequency	Percent	Valid Percent	Cumulative Percent
Disagree	1	7	7	7
Neutral	6	4.0	4.0	4.7
Agree	70	46.7	46.7	53.1
Strongly Agree	73	48.7	48.7	100.0
Total	150	100	100	

According to Table 4.15 3b, 0.7% of participants disagreed, 4.0% were neutral, 46.7% agreed, and 48.7% strongly agreed that a successful dealership depended on business location (N = 150). Business location was positively related to number of previous dealers. It would appear that a bad location would be synonymous with frequent dealer turnover.

Figure 4.15: Location and business success

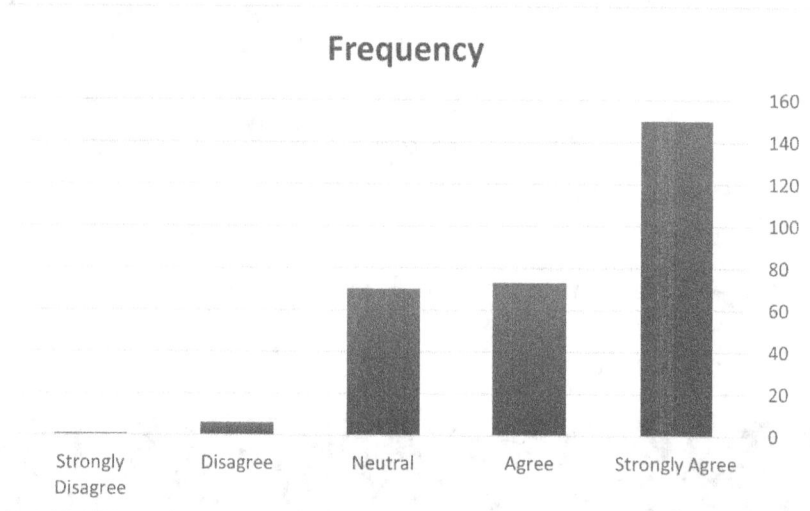

Table 4.16: Business management/entrepreneurship skills and business success

Business entrepreneurship skill

	Frequency	Percent	Valid Percent	Cumulative Percent
Disagree	3	2.0	2.0	2.0
Neutral	11	7.3	7.3	9.3
Agree	66	44.0	44.0	53.3
Strongly Agree	70	46.7	46.7	100.0
Total	150	100	100	

According to Table 4.16, 3c, 2% of participants disagreed, 7.3% were neutral, 44% agreed, and 46.7% strongly agreed that a successful dealer required business entrepreneurship skills (N = 150).

Figure 4.16: Business management/entrepreneurship skills and business success

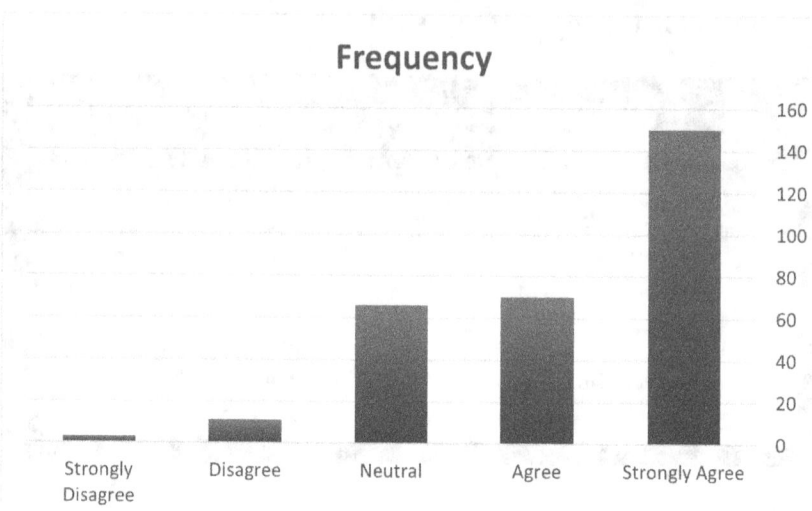

Table 4.17: Multiple business on site, customer service and business success

Multiple businesses on the site and good customer service

	Frequency	Percent	Valid Percent	Cumulative Percent
Strongly Disagree	2	1.3	1.3	1.3
Disagree	4	2.7	2.7	4.0
Neutral	3	2.0	2.0	6.0
Agree	53	35.3	35.3	41.3
Strongly Agree	88	58.7	58.7	100.0
Total	150	100	100	

According to Table 4.17, 3d, 1.3% of participants strongly disagreed, 2.7% disagreed, 2% were neutral, 35.3% agreed, and 58.7% strongly agreed that a successful dealership required multiple businesses on site, and good customer service (N = 150).

It has already been established that there is a positive correlation between multiple businesses on the site and the size of the profit margin and the risky nature of the business. Because fuel profit margins are very low, it is increasingly becoming a must to incorporate adequate non-fuel related business.

Figure 4.17: Multiple businesses on site, customer service and business success

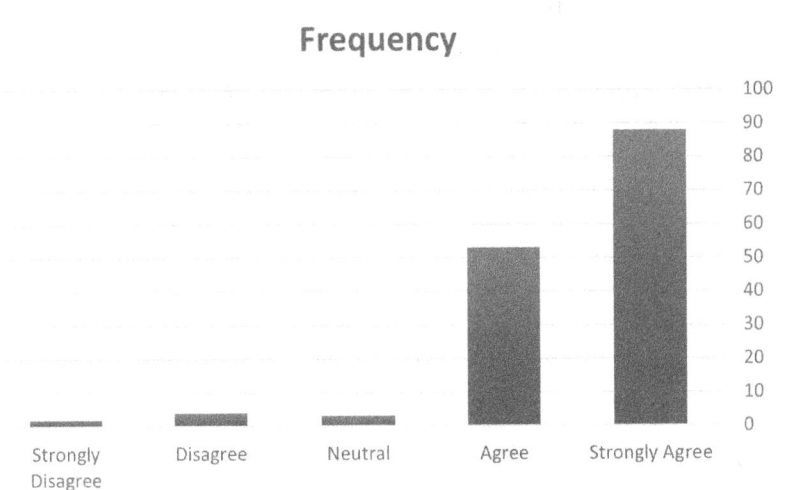

Table 4.18: Risk management skills and business success

	Frequency	Percent	Valid Percent	Cumulative Percent
Disagree	7	4.7	4.7	4.7
Neutral	10	6.7	6.7	11.3
Agree	58	38.7	38.7	50.0
Strongly Agree	75	50.0	50.0	100.0
Total	150	100	100	

According to Table 4.18, 4.7% of participants disagreed, 6.7% were neutral, 38.7% agreed, and 50% strongly agreed that a successful dealer required risk management skills (N = 150). The sector is a high risk sector. The profit margins are very low. A positive correlation was found between the need for risk management skills and adequate insurance/security cover (r =0.1, N= 150).

Figure 4.18: Risk management skills and business success

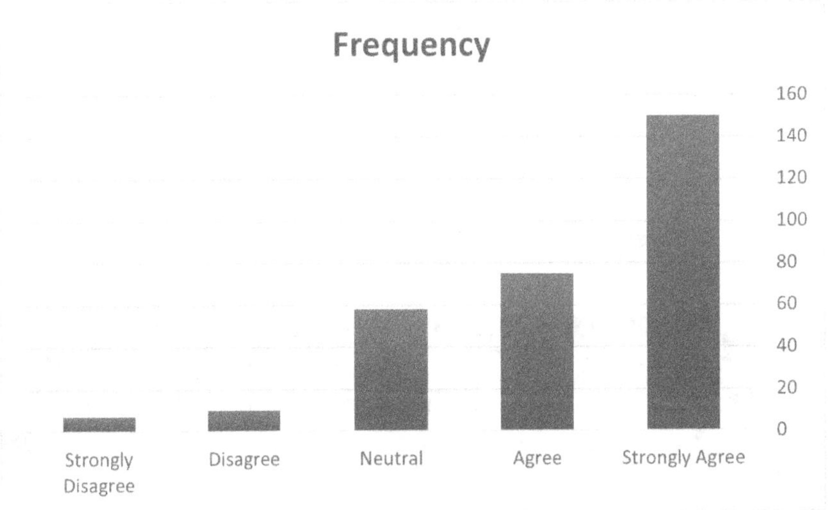

Frequency

[Bar chart showing frequencies across categories: Strongly Disagree (very low), Disagree (very low), Neutral (~60), Agree (~80), Strongly Agree (~150). Y-axis ranges from 0 to 160.]

The majority of the participants affirmed the above key success factors. Neglecting these key factors can lead to dealer collapse. For instance, poor risk management, poor site location and lack of adequate non-fuel related business have been reported under literature review as circumstances that can cause business closure. There was good correlation between the findings and what was reported under literature review.

Section E of the research

The purpose of this section was to determine the major root causes of fuel franchise business collapse. Major failure factors were considered under this section. The research question under this section was as follows:

What are the major root causes of fuel franchise business collapse/giving up?

Participants considered five factors under this question. Each factor is listed on top of a frequency table hereunder. Listed below is how the participants rated each factor.

Table 4.19: Financial indiscipline and poor risk management

Financial indiscipline and poor risk management

	Frequency	Percent	Valid Percent	Cumulative Percent
Strongly Disagree	4	2.7	2.7	2.7
Disagree	2	1.3	1.3	4.0
Neutral	24	16.0	16.0	20.0
Agree	58	38.7	38.7	58.7
Strongly Agree	62	41.3	41.3	100.0
Total	150	100	100	

According to Table 4.19, 4a, 2.7% of participants strongly disagreed, 1.3% disagreed, 16% were neutral, 38.7% agreed, and 41.3% strongly agreed that one of the root causes of fuel franchise business collapse is financial indiscipline and poor risk management (N = 150).

It was interesting to note that there was positive correlation between the above factor and previous dealers. Although dealer turnover could be due to many reasons, the fact that there appeared to be a correlation between financial indiscipline and poor risk management on one hand and dealer turnover on the other hand implied that the above factor could cause business collapse leading to a search for another dealer ($r = 0.34$, $N = 150$).

Figure 4.19: Financial indiscipline and poor risk management

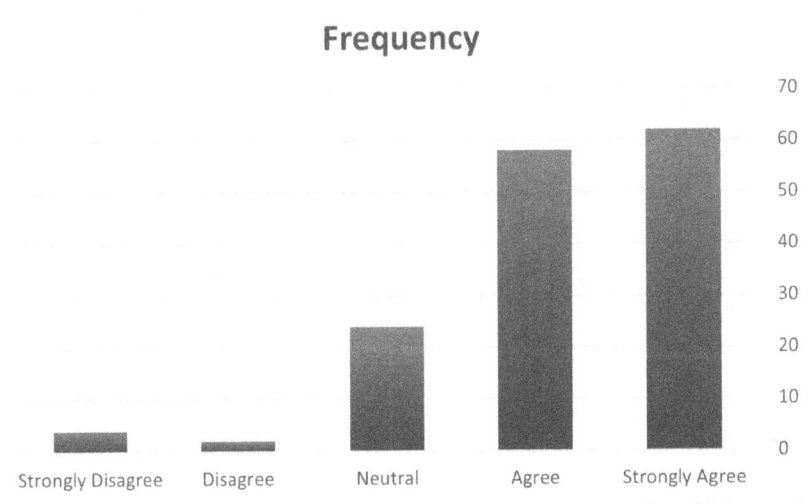

Table 4.20: Low business profitability

Impact of thin margins

	Frequency	Percent	Valid Percent	Cumulative Percent
Strongly Disagree	2	1.3	1.3	1.3
Disagree	14	9.3	9.3	10.7
Neutral	20	13.3	13.3	24.0
Agree	63	42.0	42.0	66.0
Strongly Agree	51	34	34	100.0
Total	150	100	100	

According to Table 4.20, 1.3% of participants strongly disagreed, 9.3% disagreed, 13.3% were neutral, 42% agreed, and 34% strongly agreed that one of the root causes of fuel franchise business collapse is low business profitability (N = 150).

From the above frequency tables in the previous sections, a correlation was established around this factor. It could not be denied that this factor has a positive correlation with dealer turnover meaning that it can cause business collapse. Further, it has been established that because of low business profitability, the need for adequate non fuel related business on the site as strategy is critical.

Figure 4.20: Low business profitability

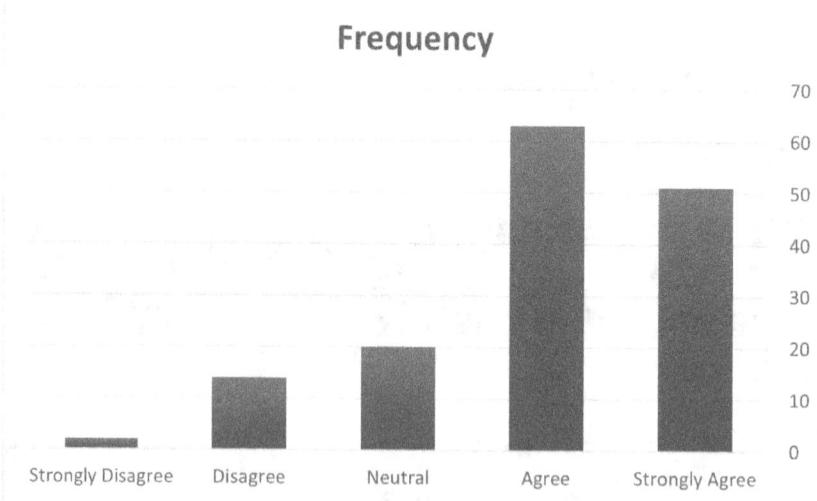

Table 4.21: Poor site location

Choice of location for petrol station

	Frequency	Percent	Valid Percent	Cumulative Percent
Strongly Disagree	3	2.0	2.0	2.0
Disagree	4	2.7	2.7	4.7
Neutral	17	11.3	11.3	16.0
Agree	69	46.0	46.0	62.0
Strongly Agree	57	38	38	100.0
Total	150	100	100	

According to Table 4.21, 2% of participants strongly agreed, 2.7% disagreed, 11.3% were neutral, 46% agreed, and 38% strongly agreed that one of the root causes of fuel franchise business collapse was poor site location (N = 150).

Poor site location can lead to business closure, hence a positive correlation with dealer turnover. Interestingly, a positive correlation ($r = 0.113$, N=150) between poor site location and multiple businesses on site and good customer service was found. It would appear that the bad the location, the more investment must be in non-fuel related business and customer service so as attract more customer patronage.

Figure 4.21: Poor site location

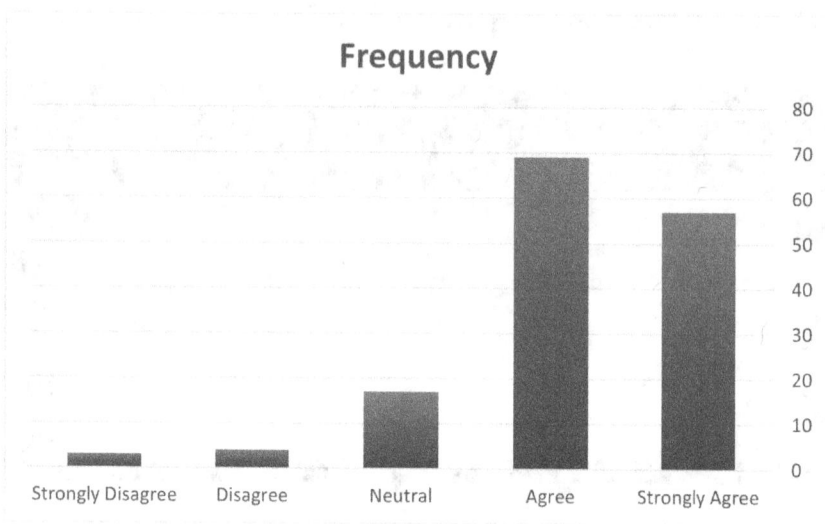

Table 4.22: Failure to manage the dealership agreement

Impact of breaching the dealership agreement

	Frequency	Percent	Valid Percent	Cumulative Percent
Disagree	7	4.7	4.7	4.7
Neutral	15	10	10	14.7
Agree	54	36.0	36.0	50.7
Strongly Agree	74	49.3	49.3	100.0
Total	150	100	100	

According to Table 4.22, 4.7% of participants disagreed, 10% were neutral, 36% agreed, and 49.3% strongly agreed that one of the root causes of fuel franchise business collapse was failure to manage the franchise/dealership agreement (N =

150).

If a dealership agreement is not managed well, it can be terminated leading to business collapse in cases where the petrol station is not dealer owned. This could be seen in a positive correlation that was established between a number of previous dealers and failure to manage the franchise agreement. The more the failure to manage the agreement, the more likely dealer change will take place (r =0.128, N =150).

Figure 4.22: Failure to manage the dealership agreement

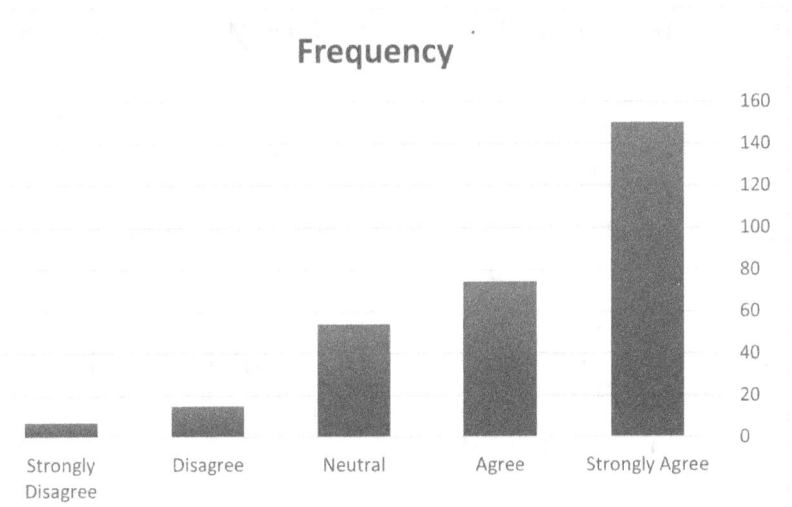

Table 4.23: Inadequate non-fuel business

Inability to incorporate sufficient non-fuel business on the site

	Frequency	Percent	Valid Percent	Cumulative Percent
Strongly Disagree	1	7	7	7
Disagree	7	4.7	4.7	5.3
Neutral	24	16.0	16.0	21.3
Agree	53	35.3	35.3	56.7
Strongly Agree	65	43.3	43.3	100.0
Total	150	100	100	

According to Table 4.23, 4e, 0.7% strongly disagreed, 4.7% disagreed, 16% were neutral, 35.3% agreed and 43.3% strongly agreed that one of the root causes of fuel franchise business collapse is the inability to incorporate sufficient non-fuel businesses on site (N = 150).

Previous correlation in the earlier sections have revealed that incorporating adequate non-fuel related business is a good strategy due to the meagre size of the profit margin in the sector. It follows that inability to implement this strategy can affect business and in some cases can force business collapse leading to a search for a new dealer. This has been confirmed by a positive correlation between number of previous dealers and the above factor under consideration (r = 0.73, N =150).

Figure 4.23: Inadequate non-fuel business

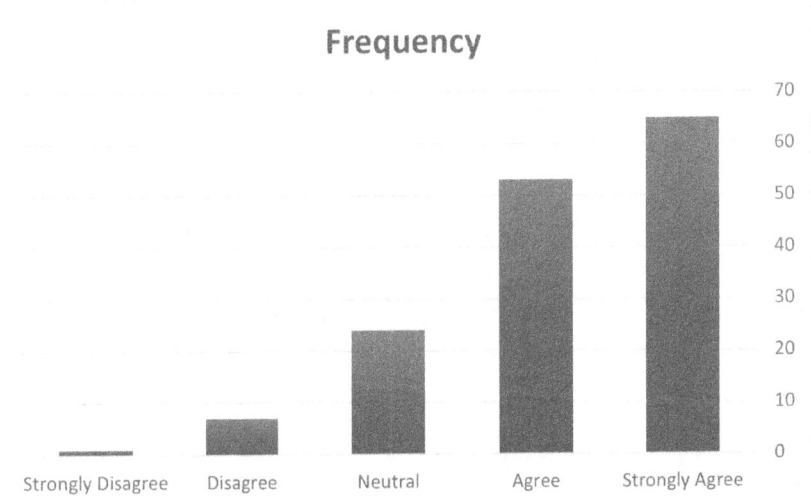

Interpretation and discussion

From Table 4.1, it was interpreted that the sector was male dominated. Of the participants interviewed, 82% were male and the rest were women. The industry bodies and in particular the Department of Minerals and Energy ought to find ways of promoting gender equity in the sector. It could be argued however that because of industry specific challenges, women may have tended to avoid participating in the sector. On the other hand, high entry barriers such as high capital requirements may be hampering women participation. It is a challenge for most women to access huge capital outlay.

From Table 4.2, only 38.1% of the participants had more than 10 years' experience in the sector. A critical analysis of this statistic could imply that there are few long-term investors in the sector. It could be that dealers retire early or cannot continue for various reasons. It is highly probable that sector challenges hamper long term plans. The majority of dealers appear to have been in the sector for less than 10 years. Although there are a few new stations being constructed and requiring new dealers, it could also be that frequent dealer turnover is responsible for this.

From Table 4.3, it can be concluded that there is hardly a dealer who took over a station that has not been run before by previous dealers. This implies that there is high dealer turnover in the sector. This confirms the high number of petrol stations being advertised. From the above two paragraphs, it could be understood that there are challenges in the industry affecting the dealers.

Regarding sector challenges, most of the dealers interviewed overwhelmingly confirmed the following as major challenges in the sector:

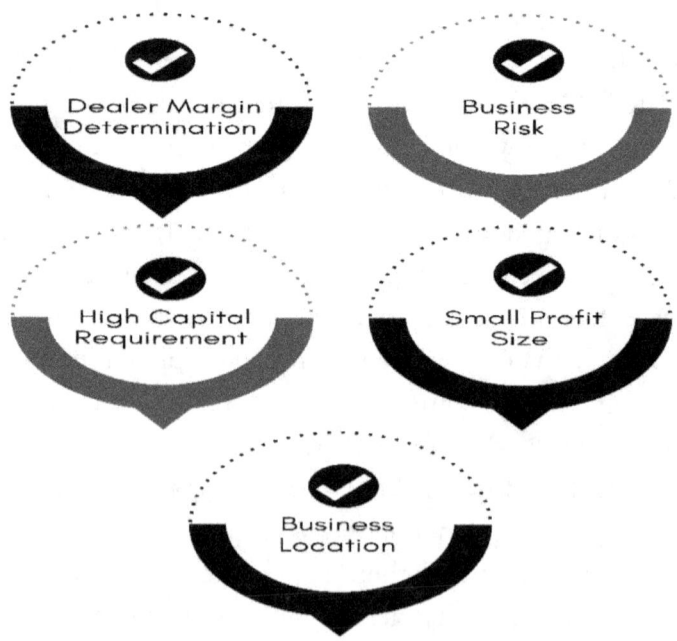

These challenges are highlighted in Tables 4.4, 4.5, 4.6, 4.7 and 4.8. It can be argued that these challenges have contributed to high dealer turnover and the decline in the number of petrol stations.

Despite the foregoing, the industry is still active and turning over billions of Rands per year. It can be understood that there are dealers who have mastered the art of dealing with sector challenges. Most of the participants interviewed reported that they dealt with the above challenges by:

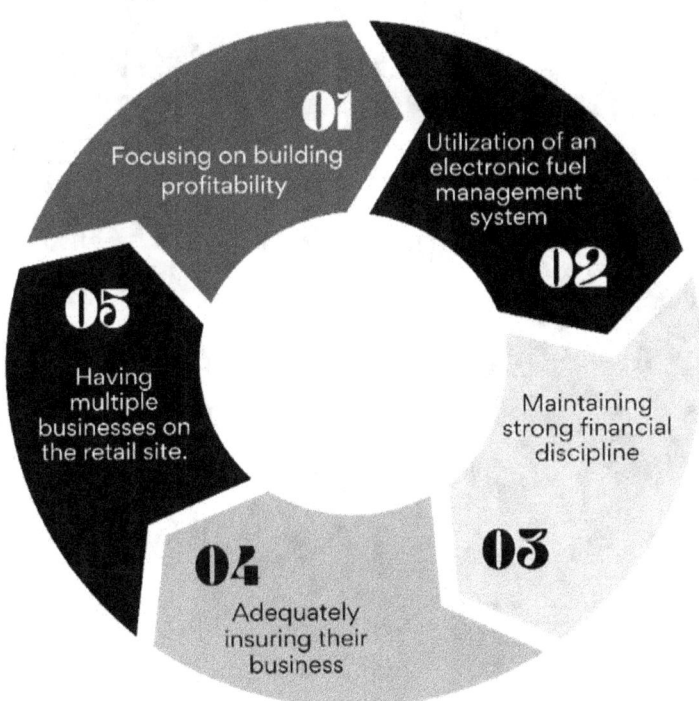

This strategy appears to be in tandem with the observations from secondary data. Various dealer responses regarding how they dealt with the above challenges are listed in Tables 4.9, 4.10, 4.11, 4.12, and 4.13.

In every industry, there are key success and failure factors. One of the objectives of the study was to establish what it takes to be successful in the sector.

On average, more than 65% of the participants reported the following as key business success drivers:

Without paying adequate attention to the above factors, it is difficult to survive in this sector. These primary findings appear to agree with literature review.

On the other hand, most of the participants reported the following as major causes of business collapse:

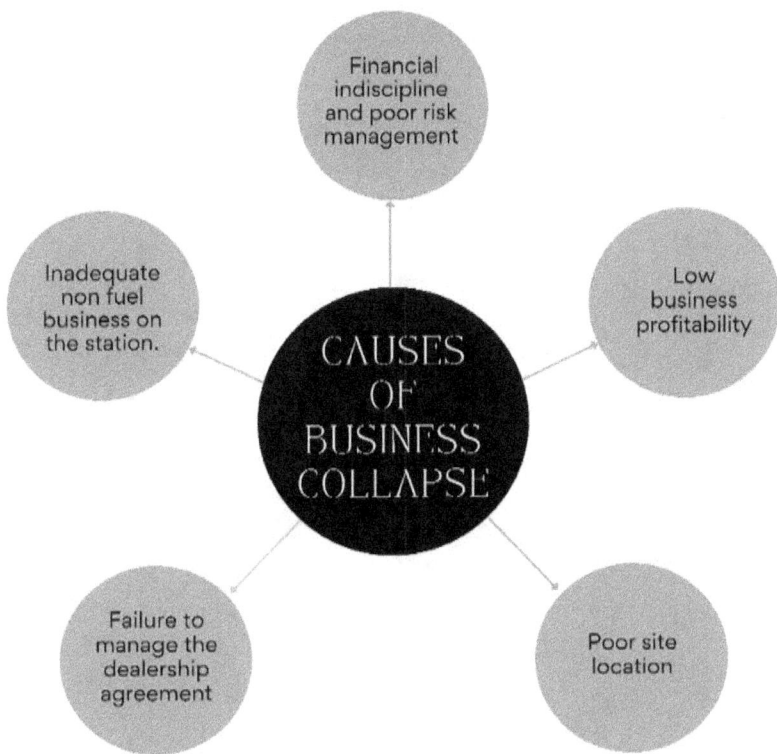

This is not the first study to report low business profitability in the sector. As can be seen from the background to the research, the Department of Energy of the Republic of South Africa commissioned a study in 2004. It was discovered that only 40% of petrol stations operated profitably with regard to selling fuel.

CHAPTER 5:

CONCLUSIONS AND RECOMMENDATIONS

5.1 Introduction

The conclusions elaborated below are based on the results of the research and existing body of literature relevant to the topic. Recommendations were made from the observations made in the research.

5.2 Findings from the study

The primary aim of the study was to identify key success and failure factors in the retail fuel sector in the Gauteng Province, South Africa. The specific objectives were as follows:

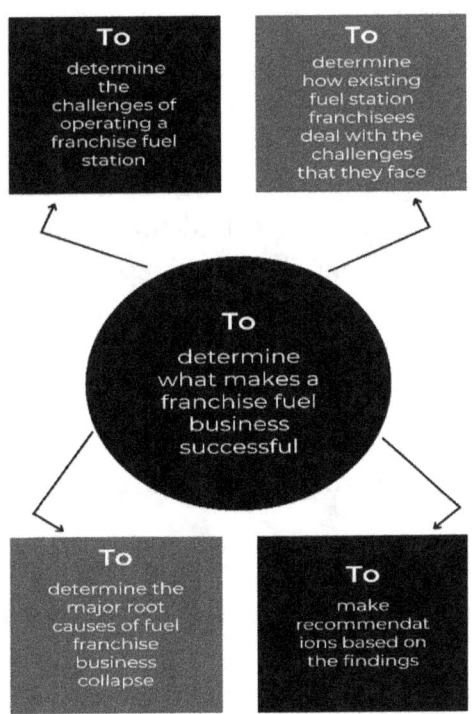

These specific objectives were to be achieved through analysis of both secondary and primary data. The study revealed that the industry has several challenges such as dealer inability to freely revise the pump prices, high capital requirements, small profit margins, high risks and business depending on location. Of the participants interviewed, the majority agreed that these were sector challenges.

In addition, it was determined how existing fuel dealers deal with challenges. The majority of participants reported that they dealt with the challenges by maintaining a focus on building profitability, employing a fuel management system to help them with accounting and monitoring product movement on the site, deploying strong financial discipline. Furthermore, they have adequate insurance cover to mitigate the high risk nature of the business and multiple businesses on the petrol station.

Key success factors in the industry include strong financial management skills, business location, entrepreneurial skills, risk management skills, incorporation of strong non fuel related business and good customer care. Most participants interviewed reported financial indiscipline and poor risk management, low business profitability, poor site location, failure to manage the dealership agreement and inability to incorporate adequate non fuel related business as major causes of business collapse in the sector.

5.2.1 Findings from the literature review

From literature review, it was observed that the number of petrol stations had been declining due to various reasons not just in South Africa but also in some other leading countries such as the United Kingdom (UK) and United States of America

(USA). The study established the challenges responsible for the decline. The challenges include financial indiscipline and poor risk management, dealer inability to determine own margin, high risks and capital requirement.

It was found that there were many petrol stations being advertised for sale both on internet and in print media. Although it can be argued that new ones are being built and also being advertised, it is clear from the adverts that most of the stations being advertised are old ones. The meaning of this is that dealers are either giving up on their own or they are losing the stations due to other reasons such as loss of capital. It was also established that there are some thousands of petrol stations still operating viably. For them to be viable they had found a way of dealing with the challenges at hand. The high dealer turnover was confirmed by the primary findings showing that there are few long term investors in the sector.

From the study conducted by Peacock Consulting on 74 BP petrol stations around South Africa, the importance of incorporating adequate non fuel related business on the petrol station was underscored. This is one of the strategies used to maximise earnings from the site and compensate for the low profit margin on fuel.

As reported under literature review, the sector has industry bodies such as the South African Petroleum Industries Association (SAPIA) and Fuel Retailers Association (FRA) representing the interests of oil marketers and fuel franchisees respectively. My finding was that these bodies are crucial to fostering and protecting the interests of their respective members. They champion the interests of their members in a highly regulated market. With the kind of challenges established from the primary study, dealer representation by the FRA is extremely important.

From literature, it was found that the government through the Department of Minerals and Energy (DME) conducted a study in 2004 to establish the profitability of retail business. It was found that only 40% of fuel stations were profitable regarding selling fuel. This reality was confirmed by this research in that most participants interviewed reported that the profit margin was very small leading to high changes of loss making.

As correctly observed by Hewitt 2012, gas station business is extraordinarily competitive. Business owners that select an excellent location and run an inviting convenience store, a car wash and an auto mechanic shop can turn a steady profit. Gas stations have some complexities including environmental issues related to gasoline storage that make it challenging. In addition, profit margins on petrol can be less than 10%, making it important to develop alternative revenue streams.

Furthermore, it was observed that there was little secondary information such as books and similar studies about the industry. Because of lack of adequate information especially from independent sources, It can be argued that there are some investors who enter this sector without adequate due diligence and knowledge of how to evaluate a franchise opportunity.

5.2.2 Findings from the Primary Research

5.2.2.1 Demographic information

5.2.2.1.1 Gender involvement in the industry

From the findings, it was established that the industry is male dominated. Out of the 150 participants, 82% are male while 18% are female. This could be because of the intense challenges typical of this industry. Additionally, it could be part of a wider gender imbalance participation in the national economy. Further, it could be due to gender bias at dealer selection stage. The industry is capital intensive as seen in the outcome of this study.

5.2.2.2 Years of experience in fuel business

Findings revealed that 38.1 % had been in the industry for at least 10 years. 29.5% had been in the sector for a period ranging from 6-10 years compared to 19.7% who had been 2 and 5 years' experience in the industry. The study showed that 12.9% had 0 to 1 year experience in the industry.
A critical analysis of these figures revealed that the majority of participants (about 60%) had less than ten years' experience in the industry. For an old industry to have these kinds of figures, it revealed a worrying underlining trend. It could be argued that most entrepreneurs do not last long in this industry. This could be a possible pointer to the decline in the number of petrol stations or dealer turnover reported under literature review and research background.

5.2.2.3 Number of previous dealers

From the findings, 24.1 % of participants reported that there was 0-1 dealer before they took over a petrol station. Forty point nine percent reported that there had been 2-5 dealers in the station before them. Twenty seven percent reported that there had been 6-10 dealers before them while 8% reported that at least 10 dealers are believed to have run the station before them.
The disturbing reality about these findings was that there appeared to be a high dealer turnover in the sector. Combined

67.9% participants (40.9% + 27%) revealed that their stations hand changed hands from 2 to 10 different owners. These figures appeared to suggest that there were very few stations which are first hand. All these findings are pointers to the challenges faced in this heavily regulated industry and a further confirmation of findings from literature review.

5.2.2.4 Challenges of operating in the retail fuel business

The first objective in this study was "to determine the challenges of operating a franchise fuel station." Participants were asked to reveal their feelings regarding five statements listed below:

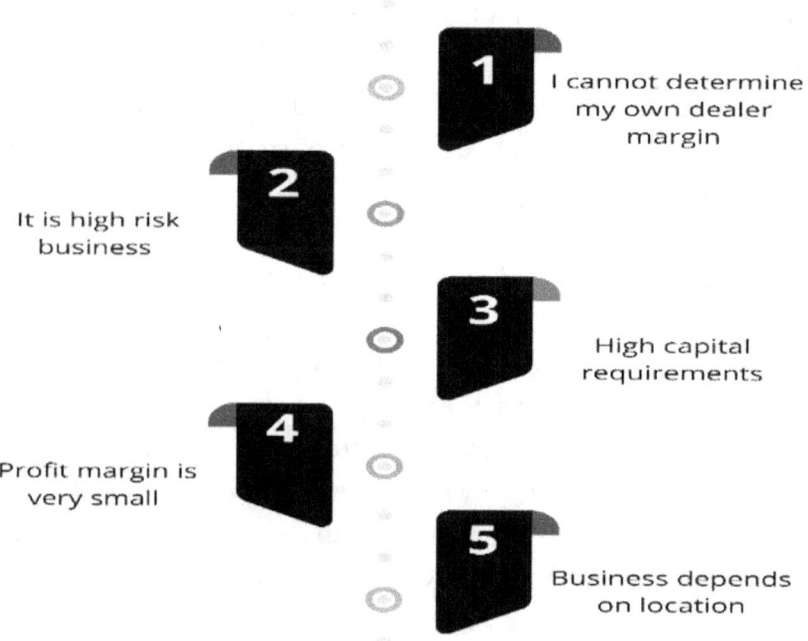

The summary of the responses to the statement "I cannot determine my own margin was as follows:"

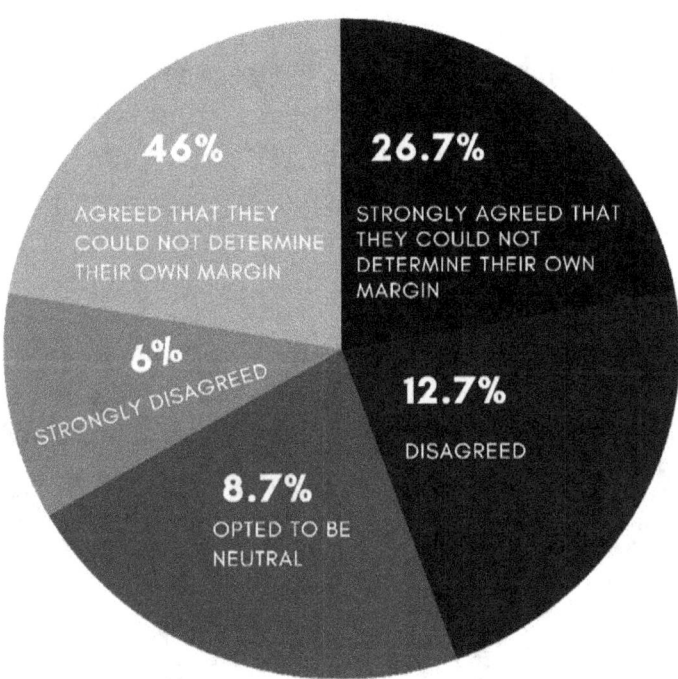

As can be seen from the above percentages 72.7% (46% + 26.7%) felt that the issue of margin adjustment in the retail sector is beyond their control. This is consistent with literature review indicating a heavy hand of government regulation in price fixing in the sector. However, government does not regulate the price of diesel at least in South Africa at the time of the study.

This partial benefit of self-regulation is however controlled by oil companies through their offering of the recommended selling price for diesel. It could be argued that some dealers want to be in good books with their principals hence enforcing the recommended selling price even though government does not regulate the diesel selling price. This could account for some participants who felt that they possessed leverage to adjust the price in some cases.

From the foregoing, it can be deduced that the issue of lack of freedom to adjust pump prices is a real challenge in the retail sector and a confirmation of findings from literature review that Government controls the prices in the sector.

The summary of the responses to the statement, "it is high risk business was follows:

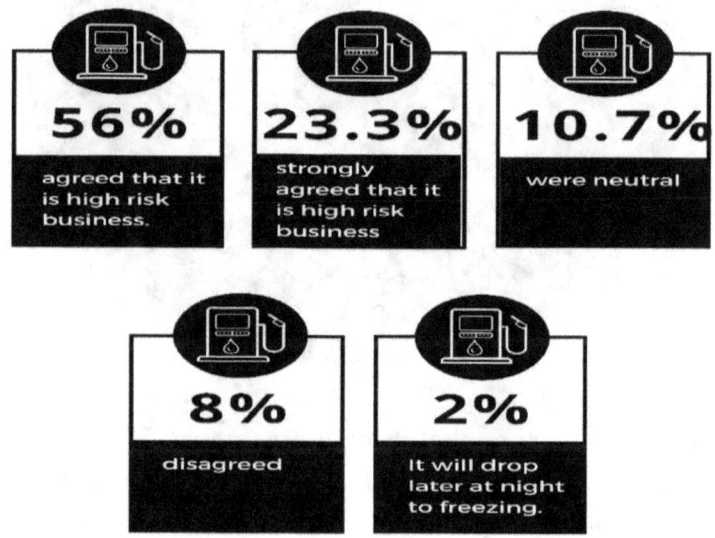

As can be seen from the above figures 79.3% (56% + 23.3%) of the participants felt that retail fuel business is a high risk business. Even the 10.7% that opted to be neutral does not help matters. Once again this can be a reason there have been reduction of petrol stations, high dealer turn over and few long term dealers as can be seen from the demographics in section 5.2. Therefore, it can be concluded that retail fuel business is a high risk business.

The summary of the responses to the statement, "high capital requirement is was follows:

As can be seen from the above figures 77.3% (56% + 21.3%) of the participants felt that retail fuel business is a high capital requirement zone. Indeed, for one to qualify for consideration to operate a fuel franchise, adverts indicate amounts in millions of rands. For the majority of the participants to feel this way, it means that this is a real challenge for most entrepreneurs. It can therefore be deduced that high capital requirements is one of the challenges in this sector.

The summary of the responses to the statement, "profit margin is very small" was as follows:

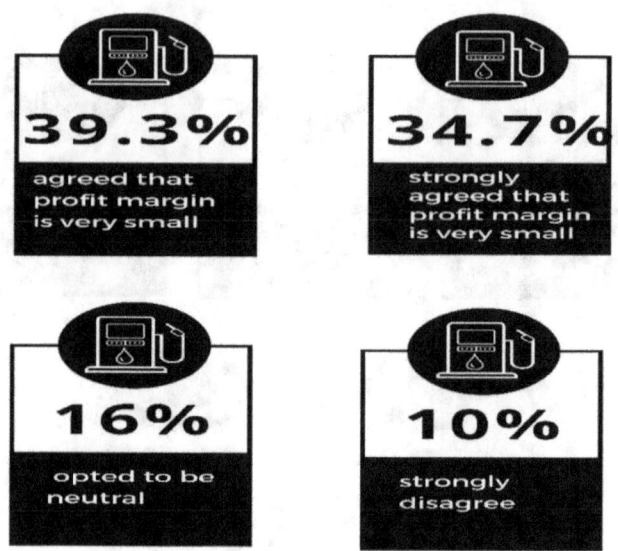

As can be seen from the above figures 77.3% (56% + 21.3%) of the participants felt that retail fuel business is a high capital requirement zone. Indeed, for one to qualify for consideration to operate a fuel franchise, adverts indicate amounts in millions of rands. For the majority of the participants to feel this way, it means that this is a real challenge for most entrepreneurs. It can therefore be deduced that high capital requirements is one of the challenges in this sector.

As can be seen from the above figures 64% (39.3% + 34.7%) felt that profit margins are very small. Although there is a good number of participants who opted to be neutral, it can be deduced that the majority of the participants felt that the size of the profit margin is a real challenge in the retail fuel sector. This challenge is made worse by the fact that margin adjustments are at the stroke of government wishes. Even if prices are increased, it does not necessarily translate into an increase of dealer margins. From the feedback received, the size of the profit margin qualifies to be listed as a challenge.

The summary of the responses to the statement, "business depends on location" was as follows:

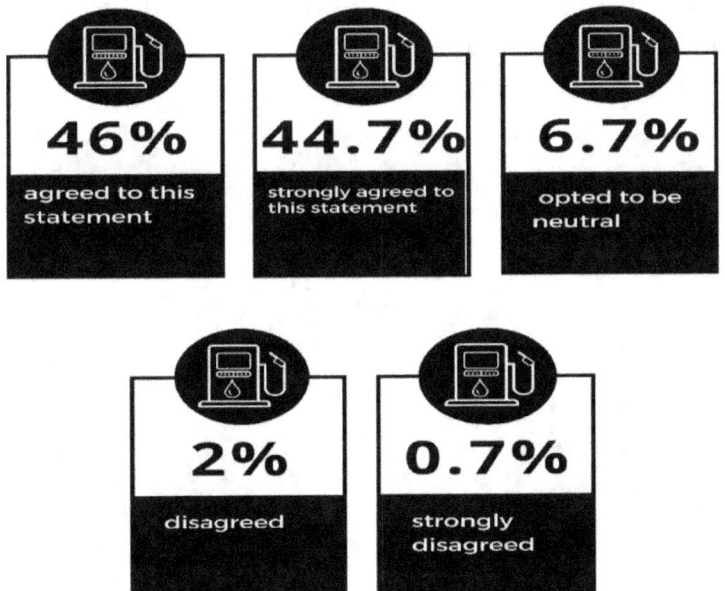

As can be seen from the above figures 90.7% (46% + 44.7%) felt that fuel business depends on location. This is an overwhelming response. It is also a confirmation of the observations in literature review which indicate that business location is a critical consideration for business success in the sector. The small number of those who remained neutral or rejected the statement could be because they operate petrol stations in locations where motorists have little choice as customers cannot do without fuel.

Therefore, it has been established that retail fuel business depends on location. It is a challenge that prospective dealers must pay attention to especially that it is not easy to find an ideal location.

5.2.2.5 Dealing with challenges in the retail sector

The second objective in the study was, "to determine how existing fuel station franchisees deal with the challenges that they face." Participants were asked to disclose their feelings with regard to five statements listed below:

The summary of responses to the statement "Iam focused on building profitability" was as follows:

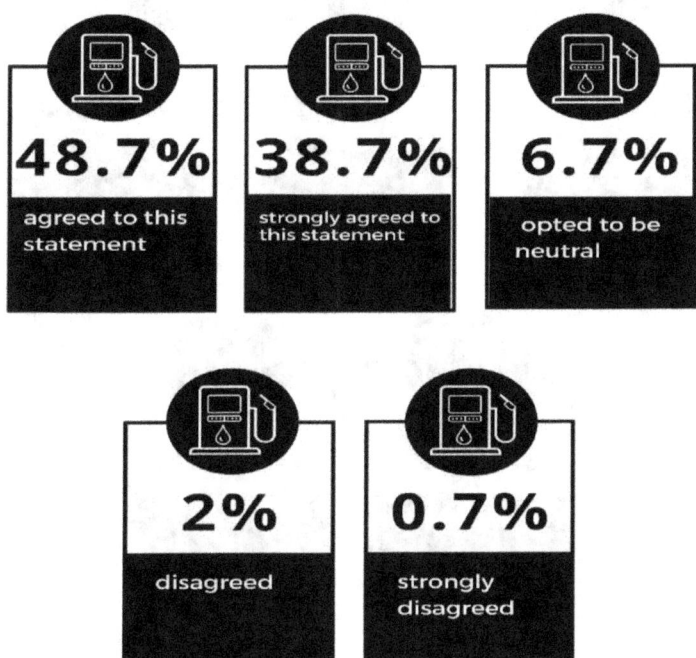

As can be seen from the figures 87.4% (48.7% + 38.7%) stated that they delt with some challenges in the sector by remaining focused on building profitability. This is a survival capability due to the small size of the profit margin whose adjustment is beyond their control.

The results reveal that 2% and 0.7% appear to have problems with maintaining a focus to build profitability. May be they are overwhelmed by business challenges. From the above figures, it can be deduced that existing fuel dealers focus on building profitability in order to survive the harsh retail environment.

The summary of responses to the statement "I have an electronic fuel management system" was as follows:

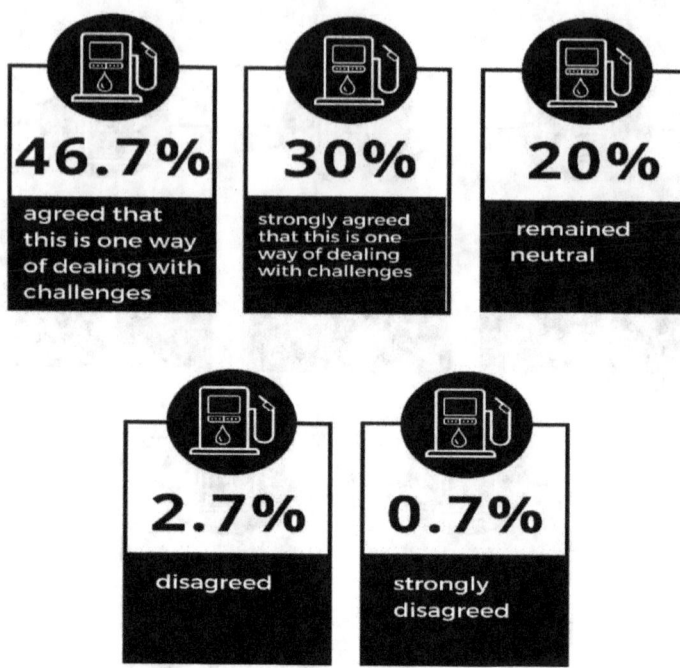

A fuel management system helps with electronic monitoring of stock in order to control re-order quantities and avoid stock outs. Further, it helps with easy stock reconciliation and balancing of sales. Additionally, it helps with control of product losses by cutting the dispensing of fuel when the exact amount order is pumped. In old equipment, this is not the case.

As can be seen from the above figures 76.7% (46.7% + 30%), the majority of participants felt that having a fuel management system is one of the ways of dealing with challenges in the retail fuel business. This is a crucial system to have in the industry owing to its robust benefits.

The summary of responses to the statement, "I have strong

financial discipline" was as follows:

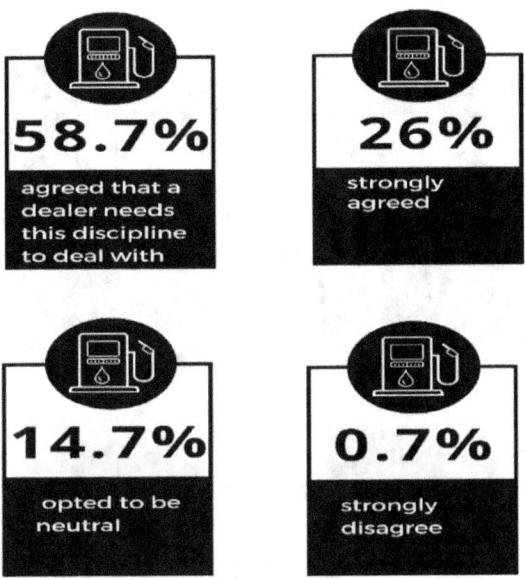

As can be seen from the statistics above, a total of 84.7% (58.7% + 26%), were in favour of financial discipline. A fuel dealer needs a lot of financial discipline to survive in this sector. The margins are low and their revision does not lie with the dealer. The sector is a cash business sector meaning that the temptation to misapply earnings is high. It is a high turnover business. Some dealers who have collapsed have collapsed on the slate of financial indiscipline. This is one way existing dealers are dealing with some challenges in the sector.

The summary of responses to the statement, "I have adequate insurance" was as follows:

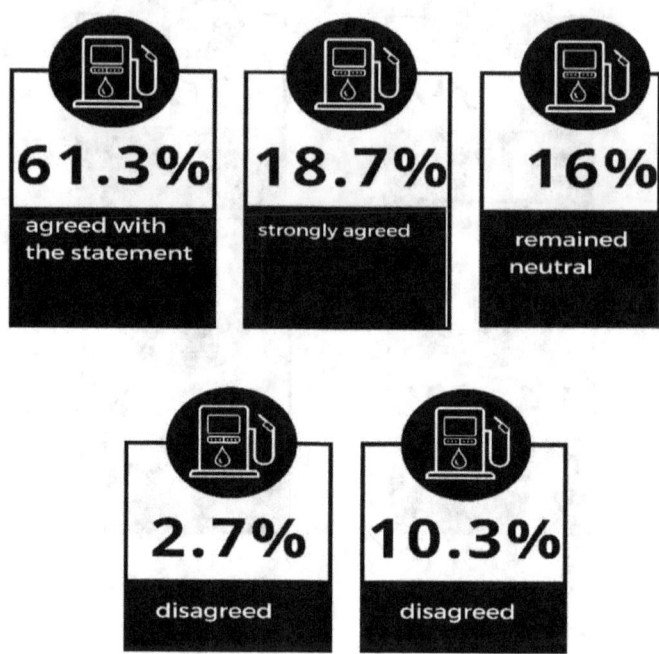

As can be seen from the above figures a combined total of 79.3% (61.3%+18.7%) agreed that they had adequate insurance. From this staggering statistic, it can be concluded; most dealers felt that protecting their business in this sector against the vagaries of life was crucial. Because, it is a high cash business, the potential for aggravated robbery is high. The potential for fire is high because fuel is highly inflammable.

It is a pit that some participants felt inadequately insured/ protected/ secured. May be they have cut down on insurance levels and security in order to maximize earnings. It could also be that they do not have CCTV camera on sight. As is typical in any survey, some participants were not sure whether they have adequate protection or not.

The summary of responses to the statement, "I have several other businesses on the site" was as follows:

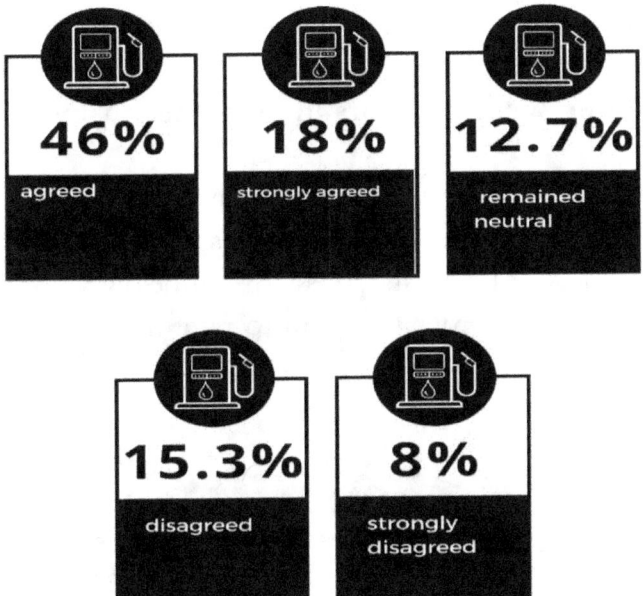

The majority of participants reported that they had other businesses on the site. Other businesses in this case refer to activities non-related to fuel sales such as car wash and convenience stores. Convenience stores have emerged as a very serious compliment in fuel business. In literature review, some dealers were quoted as making more margins and money from stores compared to fuel sales. However, this depended on location and the size of the store.

It can be concluded that this was one way most dealers were dealing with the challenge of inadequate profit margins and competition in the sector by strengthening other businesses on the site.

A combined 23.3% felt that they did not have sufficient other businesses on the retail sites. This is typical of old generation petrol stations some of which are still in existence. In those days, non-fuel business on petrol stations was not emphasized. This is evident from the size of some of the convenient stores on some sites. In some cases, there is no store at all.

5. 2.2.6 Key success factors in retail fuel business

The third objective in this study was "to investigate what makes a franchise fuel business successful." To deal with this objective, a set of five statements listed below was presented to participants in order for them to rate their feelings on the same.

The summary of responses to the statement "strong financial management skills" was as follows:

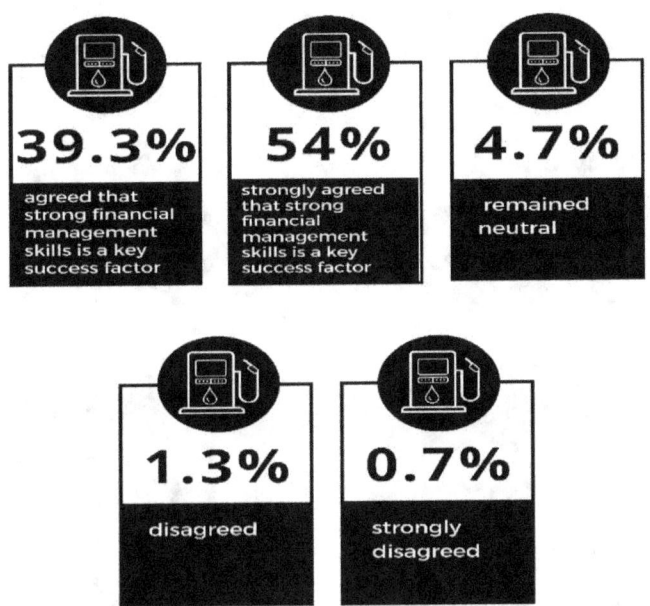

As can be seen from the above figures, a total of more than 90% of participants agreed that strong financial management skills were a key success factor in the retail fuel business. Therefore, it can be concluded that one of the things that make a franchise fuel business successful is strong financial management skills on the part of the investor.

The summary of responses to the statement "business location" was as follows:

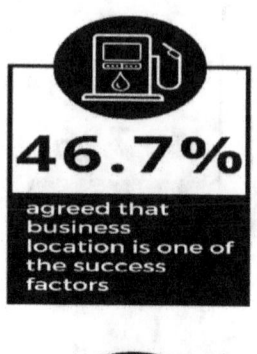

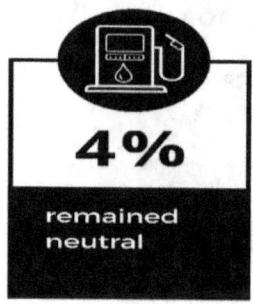

As can be seen from the above figures, a total of more than 90% of the participants rated business location as a key success factor. It can be concluded that one of the ways to succeed in this sector is settle for an appropriate location.

The summary of responses to the statement "business entrepreneurship skills" was as follows:

As can be seen from the above summary, slightly more than 90% of the participants reported business entrepreneurship skills as a key success factor.

It can therefore be concluded that entrepreneurship skills are key to the survival of fuel franchisees. They need to have a vision of where they want to be in a specific time. They need to know how to manage, control, plan and influence business direction. The summary of the responses to the statement "multiple businesses on the site and good customer service was as follows:

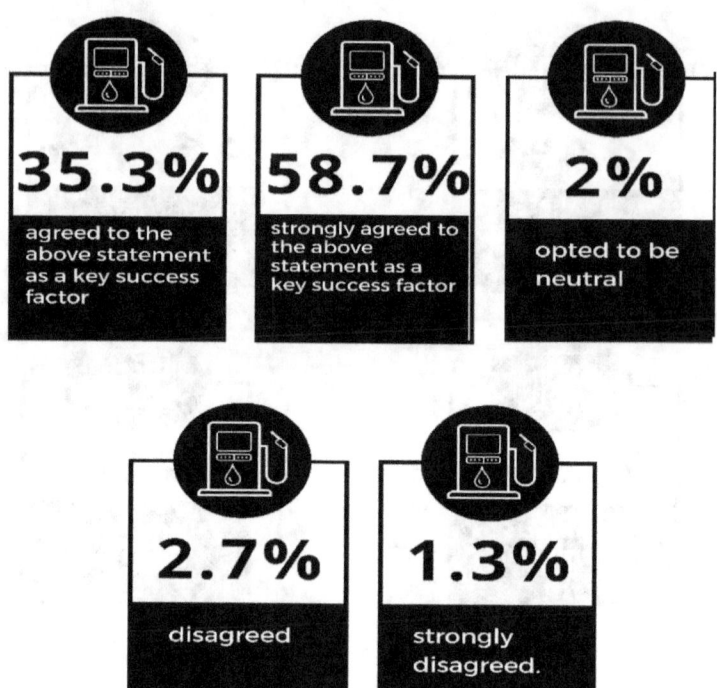

The idea of having multiple businesses on a petrol station is an emerging business aimed at optimizing earnings on the retail site. Customer service in this sector is like blood to a human being. Those who disagreed were probably running locations that were either very busy on fuel business or in areas where they have little or no competition.

From a close analysis of the feedback from the participants, it could be observed that more than 90% rated the idea of having multiple businesses on the site and customer service as a premium key success factor to the prospects of the dealer.

It can therefore be concluded that having multiple businesses and good customer service on the fuel retail site is one of the key fuel business success factors.

The summary of responses to the statement "risk management skills" was as follows:

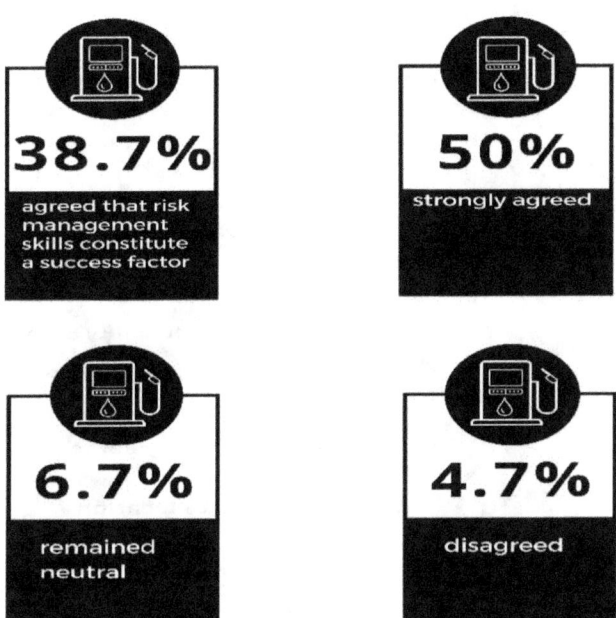

From the above figures, a total of more than 88% of the participants agreed that risk management skills were one of the key success factors in the sector. The fuel product is an inflammable material. Retail fuel business is a high cash business; hence it is vulnerable to aggravated robbery. In addition, the margins are very small. Therefore, the margin must be protected as much as possible from avoidable losses.

It can be deduced that it takes good risk management skills to be a successful fuel franchisee.

5.2.2.7 Major failure factors in the retail fuel sector

The fourth objective in this study was "to determine the major root causes of fuel franchise business collapse." To deal with this objective, a set of five statements listed below was presented to participants for them to rate their feelings:

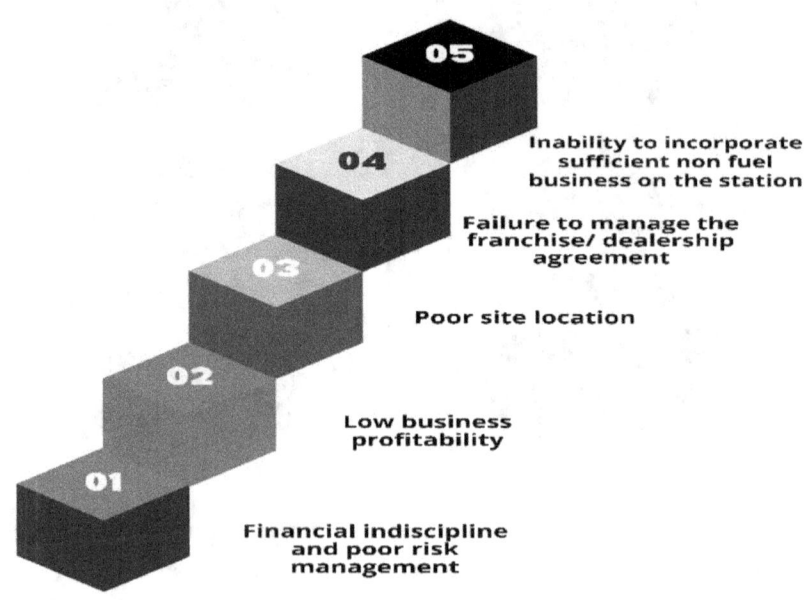

The summary of responses to the statement "financial indiscipline and poor risk management" was as follows:

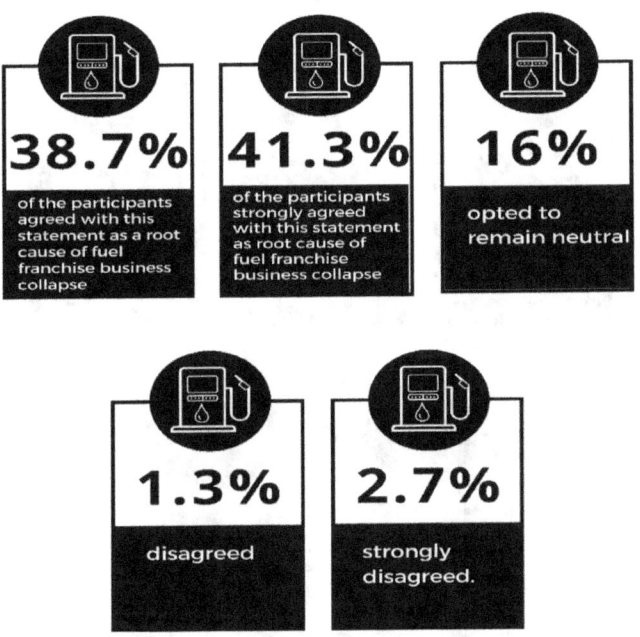

As can be seen from the above statistics, a combined total of 80% (38.7%+41.3%) of participants were in favour of the statement that financial indiscipline and poor risk management was one of the causes of fuel franchise business collapse. The small number of participants who were not in support of the statement could be of the view that even when a dealer is financially disciplined and has got good risk management skills, yet he or she can still go out of business.

From the number of participants who agreed with this statement, it can be deduced that financial indiscipline and poor risk management is one of the major causes of fuel franchise business collapse.

The summary of responses to the statement "low business profitability" was as follows:

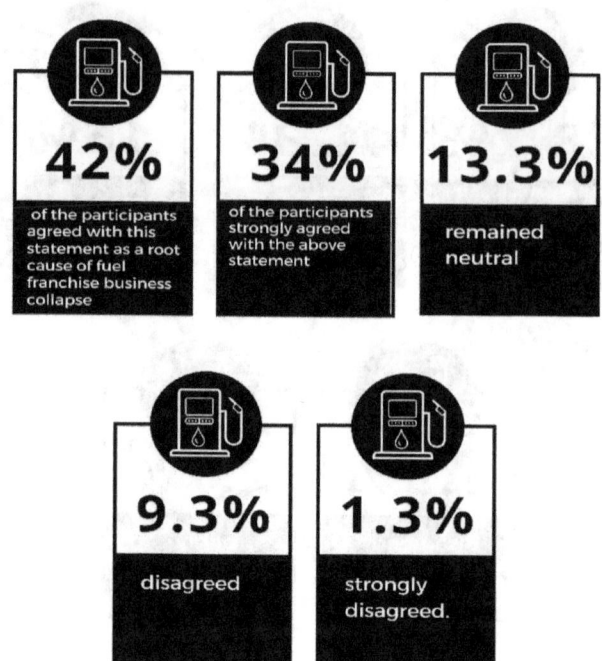

From the above statistics, a combined 76% (42%+34%) were in favour of the fact that low business profitability was one of the major root causes of fuel franchise business collapse.

It can be inferred that there is general concern in the industry on the size of the profit margin. It has been determined as one of the major root causes of fuel franchise business collapse.

The summary of responses to the statement "poor site location" was as follows:

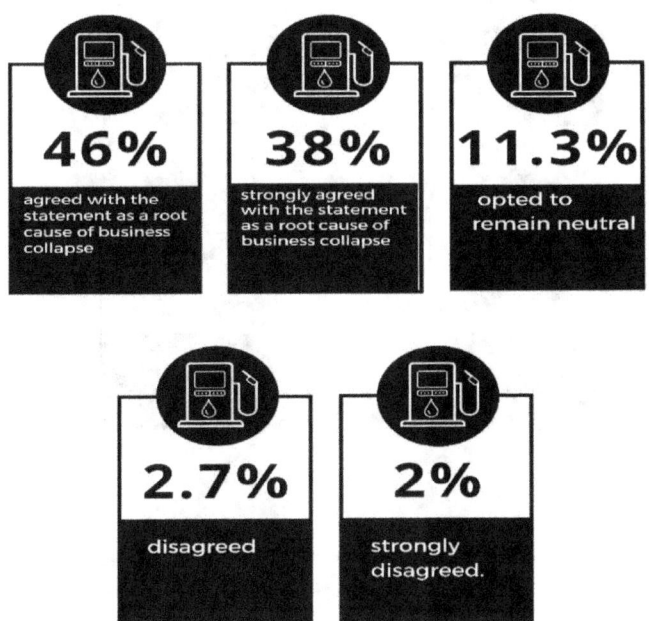

A combined total of 84% (46%+38%) agreed that poor site location was a major root cause of fuel franchise business collapse. This was very big response compared with the combined 4.7% who disagreed.

Therefore, it can be concluded that poor site location is one of the major root causes of fuel franchise business collapse.

The summary of responses to the statement "failure to manage the franchise/dealership agreement" was as follows:

 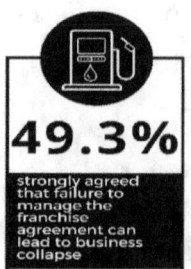

A dealership agreement is a legal document that outlines contractual obligations of the franchisee and the franchisor. From the figures above, a combined total of 85.3% (36%+49.3%) agreed that failure to manage the dealership can lead to business collapse. The franchisor can cancel the dealership agreement and evict the franchisee from the site.

On the other hand, it must be understood that there are some independent petrol stations (also called dealer owned). These are not as vulnerable as the non-independent dealers. This reality could be seen in the 4.7% and 10% who disagreed with this statement and probably those who remained neutral.

The summary of responses to the statement "inability to incorporate sufficient non-fuel business on the site" is as follows:

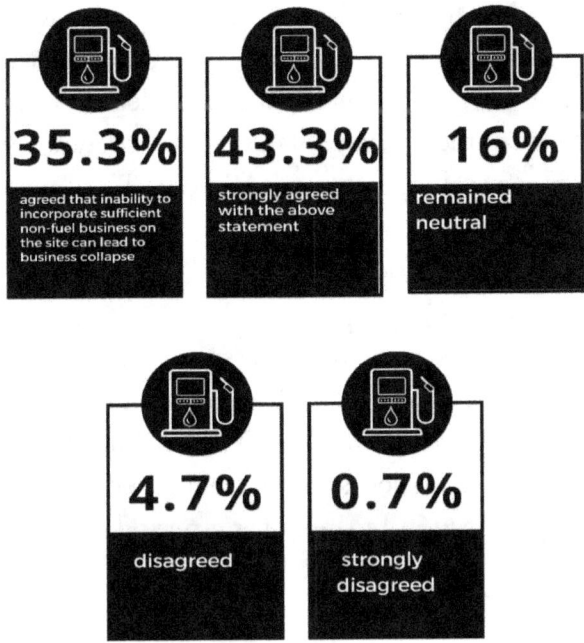

Non-fuel business is business that is not related to fuel business. It is an emerging new force aimed at optimizing earnings from a retail site. It has been realized that margins from fuel business are small and get squeezed. The Department of Energy (DoE) directly or through a regulator depending on jurisdiction is solely responsible for revising these margins. However, commodity prices in the convenience stores and other businesses on the site are not under the control of the DoE or industry regulator.

It has already been established in this study that low profit margins can lead to business collapse. There are also other factors such as competition and brand equity that can affect business. Therefore, strengthening multiple revenue streams from a site is a survival strategy. This is perhaps why more than 78% participants all agreed that inability to incorporate sufficient non-fuel business on the site was a major root cause of fuel franchise business collapse.

On the other hand, there are some stations that enjoy monopoly of location and are on busy roads. Further, dealer owned petrol stations enjoy bigger margins than non-dealer owned petrol stations. Hence some participants did not entirely agree with the above statement and others remained neutral.

5.2.2.8 Summary of findings

The findings of the study have been summarised in this chapter and compared with literature review. First and foremost, it was interesting to note that this was a male dominated industry. Additionally, the statistics showed that almost 60 % of the participants had been in business for a period not exceeding 10 years.

Given that this industry is too old for most of its dealers to have been in the sector for less than 10 years, it appeared that there had been frequent dealer turnover due to various reasons. Frequent dealer turnover can be due to business collapse, migration to other businesses or retirement. This is in line with observations made at literature review regarding dwindling numbers of petrol stations and collapse.

The literature review in this research postulated that there were industry-wide challenges that have been crippling petrol stations. Petrol stations had reduced in number. Therefore, to survive in this government regulated industry, a dealer must leverage certain factors such as incorporating non fuel related business on the petrol station. This confirmed the findings of a Peacock Consulting Survey reported under literature review. The data analysis consistently showed what an overwhelming majority felt were the challenges and what brought down the dealers.

Some factors considered such as financial indiscipline and poor risk management were double barrelled statements. Therefore, it was not easy to conclude how each sub-factor within such as statement contributed to the overall response. However, this is one of the major causes of business collapse. It was established that the sector was fraught with many challenges such as dealer inability to change margins. It was also established how most dealers dealt with these challenges by maintaining a strong focus on building profitability.

The aim of the study was to identify key success and failure factors in the retail fuel sector in the Gauteng Province of South Africa. This aim was achieved. The five objectives, which included determination of challenges of operating a franchise fuel station, were also achieved.

5.2.2.9 Conclusion

The scope of the research involved examination of secondary and primary data related to the subject matter. The aim of the study was to identify key success and failure factors in the retail fuel sector in the Gauteng Province of South Africa. The specific objectives included determination of challenges of operating a franchise fuel station, determining how existing fuel station franchisees deal with challenges, investigating what makes a franchise fuel business successful and determination of major causes of franchise business collapse. The aim and the objectives of the research were achieved.

This study was limited to Gauteng Province of South Africa. There is some scope for further studies over the entire country. In addition, it could be argued that the findings of this research are not the only success and failure factors available. Other factors such as the role of promotions, government support and oil company support can be explored. Furthermore, the impact of government control of margins needs further exploration.

However, secondary data on the retail segment appeared to be very limited.

The purpose of this book is to highlight some key success factors which are critical if a fuel trader at franchisee level is to accumulate significant returns and become a millionaire. In the same breath, the research uncovered key failure factors which serve as a grave yard in this industry. To survive in this industry, investors are encouraged to avoid this grave yard as much as possible.

Although the research was conducted a few years ago, the findings could still be valid today because regulation has continued. In addition, the findings could also be valid in most countries where regulation and franchising are still prevalent. The book has not discussed about the future of the fuel dealer in an evolving electric vehicle industry.

BIBLIOGRAPHY

Association of Small Business Development Centres (1998) Franchising 101: The Complete Guide to Evaluating, Buying and Growing Your Franchise Business. Dearborn, Chicago IL, USA.

Anonymous (2010) International Research Journal of Finance and Economics, Issue 39, Euro Journals Publishing, Inc 2010. Available from: www.eurojournals.com/finance.htm. [Accessed: 15/05/2012

Bell, J. (1999) Doing your research project. 3rd Edition, United Kingdom, Open University Press

Black, L.(April/May 2012:2) Your Business Magazine. Infocus Publishing, Cape Town, South Africa.

Brand South Africa (2012) [online]. Gauteng Province. Available from: http//www.southafrica.info/about/geography/Gauteng.htm

Campoy, A. (2008) [online]. Gas Stations Hit Skids, The Wall Street Journal, July 8, 2008. Washington DC, USA, available from: www.online.wsj.com/article/SB12153860245033105.html [Accessed: 12/01/12]

Cooper, D. and Schndler, P. (2003) Business Research Methods. 8th Edition. Boston: Brent Gordon.

Cooper, J. (2006 [online]. Top 4 Problems of Owning a Franchise. Available from: http://ezinearticles.com/?Top-4-Problems-of-Owning-a-Franchise!&id=294741 [Accessed: 1/11/12]

Chinambu, C. (2011) The Petroleum Industry in Zambia: A study on market structure and competition, United Nations, Lusaka, Zambia

Cyrus Business Brokers (2012) [online]. Fuel stations for sale. Available from: www.petrolstationsforsale.co.za [Accessed: 05/01/12]

Department of Minerals and Energy (2005a). [online] Available from: www.dme.gov.za/energy/petrol193gautfeb.htm [Accessed:05/01/12]

Dulgaro, J. (2012) [online]. How to stand out in the competitive convenience market. Available from: http://www.franchise.net.au/Article. [Accessed: 02/02/12].

Douglas, A. Lind, Robert, D. Mason and William, G. Marchal (2000). Basic Statistics for Business and Economics. 3rd Edition, United States of America, McGraw-Hill Companies.

Forecourt Times (2010). Promoting the interests of Fuel Retailers, 2010 Edition, Fuel Retailers Association, Johannesburg, South Africa

Filling Station[online]. Available from: http://en.wikipedia.org/wiki/filling_station [Accessed: 16/02/12]

Filling stations for sale (2012). [online] Available from: www.Fuelprop.co.za [Accessed: 20/01/12]

Free Online Library (2005) [online]. Petrol station closure leaves drivers stranded. Available from: www.the freelibrary.com/petro l+closure+leaves+drivers+stranded. [Accessed: 18/02/12]

FleetCube (2005) [online] Available from: http://en.wikipedia.org/wiki/filling_station [Accessed: 16/02/12]

Gonzalez, A. (2006) [online]. Gas station owners' profits hinge on thirsty customers. The Seattle Times, Seattle, USA. Available from: www.seattletimes.nwsource.com [Accessed: 30/11/11]

Graham, D. and Glaister, S. (2002). The Demand for Automobile Fuel: A survey of Elasticities. Journal of Transport Economics and Policy, 36p. 1-26

Hart, C. (2005) Doing your dissertation. New Dehli: Vistaar publications

Hewitt, J (2012:1) [online] How to Run a Gas Station Business. Available from: http://www.ehow.com/how_6127022_run-gas-station-business-html [Accessed: 08/05/2012]

Hussey, J. and Hussey, R. (1997) Business Research-A Practical Guide for Undergraduate and Postgraduate Studies, 1st Edition, Palgrave MacMillan, UK

Israel D. Glenn (2012:1) [online]. Determining Sample Size. Available from: www.edis.ifas.ufl.edu/pdoof [Accessed: 03/08/2012]

Lambert, L. (2011) Be Your Own Boss Magazine. Published by Entrepreneur Media SA, September issue, Ferndale, Johannesburg

Lee, Y. Schmidt, C (1980) A comparative location analysis of retail activity: The gasoline service station. The annals of Regional Science, 14(2)

MANCOSA (2012) Research Methodology study guide. Durban: Management College of Southern Africa.

MANCOSA (2003) Research Methodology study guide. Durban: Management College of Southern Africa.

MarketFacts (2008) [online] NPN Magazine. Available from: http://www.npnweb.com/ME2/Default.asp [Accessed: 16/02/12]

Mathews, J. Debolt, D. Percival, D. (2011) Street Smart Franchising, 2nd Edition, Entrepreneur Media, Wisconsin, USA.

Matsho, J.(2010). The Retail Petrol Industry in South Africa, University of Zululand, South Africa

Mbendi, Information for Africa (2005a) South Africa: Oil and Gas Overview [online]. Available from: www.mbendi.co.za/sapia/pdf/2005_Q1pr.xls: [Accessed 30/08/2005]

McDabe, S.(1999) Writing a dissertation proposal: Notes on the process and product. Washington

Mitchell, V. (1996. Assessing the reliability and validity of questionnaires: An empirical example, Journal of applied management studies, 5:2.

Molefe, M. M. (2006). Consumer Motivations in Forecourt Convenience Retailing in South Africa, University of Pretoria, South Africa.

Omoniyi, T. (2010). Country's sea of empty petrol stations, The Daily Trust, Nigeria, Friday, 1 January, 2010, p1

Peacock Consulting (2004). A Survey of BP Retail Fuel Stations. Site Profiling Report, Johannesburg, South Africa.

Saunders, M. Lewis, P. Thornhill, A (2003). Research Methods for Business Students. 3rd Edition: Pitman Publishing Limited, England

SAPIA (2008) Petrol and Diesel in South Africa and the impact on air quality. South African Petroleum Industry Association (SAPIA) reference guide.

Sartorius, K. Eitzen, C. and Hart, J (2007). An Examination of the variables influencing the fuel retail industry, University of Witwatersrand, Johannesburg, South Africa

Scottish Executive Publications (2005) [online]. Review of rural petrol stations grant final report. Available from: www.scotland.Gov.uk [Accessed: 21/12/06]

Smalley, S. (1999) Measuring convenience of gas stations. Appraisal Journal, October 1999

Sincich, B. M,(2008). Statistics for Business and Economics. 10th Edition, Pearson Education, inc. New Jersey, USA

Spinelli, S. Rosenberg, R. Birley, S. (2004) Franchising: Pathway to Wealth Creation, Pearson Education Inc. Upper Saddle River, NJ 07458, USA

Sully, A. (2008). [online] Mysterious death of the petrol stations, BBC News. March 24, 2008. Available from: http://news.bbc.co.uk/2/hi/uk_news/magazine/7306967.stm

Taylor, J. (2008) My Gas Station Guide [online] Available from: www.mygasstationguide.com. [Accessed: 08/05/2012]

Thomas, S. (2005) New Law May Introduce Much Needed Common Sense. Financial Mail, 181 (10): 46

Visser, A. (2005) Unmanaged deregulation to cause chaos. Gauteng Business, 18:3

Wegner, T. (2007) Applied Business Statistics. 2nd Edition, Juta and Co, Mercury Crescent, Wetton 7780, Cape Town, South Africa www.sapia.co.za[accessed: 3/08/2012]